W0081593

2 04

The Other
Side of Change

The Other Side of Change

WHO WE BECOME WHEN
LIFE MAKES OTHER PLANS

Maya Shankar

RIVERHEAD BOOKS · NEW YORK · 2026

Riverhead Books
An imprint of Penguin Random House LLC
1745 Broadway, New York, NY 10019
penguinrandomhouse.com

Grateful acknowledgment is made for permission to reprint the following:

Excerpt from "For Freckle-Faced Gerald" from *The Essential Etheridge Knight*, by Etheridge Knight, © 1986. Reprinted by permission of the University of Pittsburgh Press.

Excerpt from "What is 'Family of Origin' Work in Therapy?" on riverbanktherapy.com by Abby Birk, LMFT used with permission.

Scripture quotation on page 157 taken from the World English Bible.

Book design by Alexis Sulaimani

Library of Congress Cataloging-in-Publication Data
Names: Shankar, Maya author
Title: The other side of change : who we become when
life makes other plans / Maya Shankar.
Description: New York : Riverhead Books, 2026. |
Includes bibliographical references and index.
Identifiers: LCCN 2025008086 (print) | LCCN 2025008087 (ebook) |
ISBN 9780593713686 hardcover | ISBN 9780593713709 ebook
Subjects: LCSH: Life change events | Change (Psychology)
Classification: LCC BF637.L53 S526 2026 (print) | LCC BF637.L53 (ebook)
LC record available at https://lccn.loc.gov/2025008086
LC ebook record available at https://lccn.loc.gov/2025008087

Printed in the United States of America
1st Printing

The authorized representative in the EU for product safety and compliance is
Penguin Random House Ireland, Morrison Chambers, 32 Nassau Street,
Dublin D02 YH68, Ireland, https://eu-contact.penguin.ie.

To the Shankar and Li families

And of course to
Jimmy

Contents

Author's Note

I interviewed the people profiled in this book on repeated occasions over several years. All quotes attributed to them came from these conversations, except in a few specified cases.

Preface

There are moments in each of our lives that seem to change every-thing. A relationship ends without warning. A close friend gets into a serious accident. Routine medical tests reveal something concerning. Secrets about a loved one come to light. A job is lost. As our lives veer off course, it can feel like time is dividing into a "before" and an "after."

I had one of these experiences recently. My husband and I were on the cusp of becoming parents after years of navigating various ob-stacles and disappointments. We were brimming with relief and excitement—emotions that I imagine many parents-to-be feel. As we received one piece of good news after another, we allowed ourselves to conjure up cozy images of life with our future child: snuggling in bed and reading *Calvin and Hobbes* together or breaking out into a silly dance in our kitchen. We were finally starting a family!

Until, suddenly, we weren't.

I still remember how I felt when I heard the news. Anxiety pooled in the pit of my stomach. Ordinary sounds—like the closing of a door or a stranger's voice—were jarring, as if the volume of the outside world had been dialed up. My colleagues at work, unaware of what was going on, were emailing me about assignments that were due. I struggled to comprehend how everything was just moving forward as usual. I knew my situation was not unique, but somehow that awareness couldn't penetrate the visceral, chilling feeling that I was alone.

As the weeks and months passed, what disoriented me the most was the loss of control I felt. In everyday life, it's easy to overestimate the degree to which we influence how things turn out—psychologists call this the *illusion of control*. When a bad thing happens unexpectedly, it can shatter that illusion. As my detailed plans unraveled one by one, I became agitated by all the uncertainty that now lay ahead. There's a research study showing that people are more stressed when they think they have a 50 percent chance of receiving an electric shock than when they think they have a 100 percent chance. This finding resonates deeply with me: I like knowing how the story ends. Whenever I've faced a setback or a failure, my instinct has been to jump into action and to try to reduce any uncertainty by outworking the challenge. But what would it even mean to work harder in the context of trying to become a parent?

I'd often heard that while we can't control what happens to us, we *can* control our reaction to what happens. It's meant to be an empowering mantra, but as I grappled with my negative emotions, it registered as a platitude. Sure, it'd be great to somehow react in a more constructive manner, but how was I supposed to go about doing that? It's not like I could flip a switch in my brain that would make me feel more at peace, or more hopeful, or more certain about what to do next. I wanted to figure out how, exactly, to think and feel differently about my situation.

As I sat there, isolated in my sorrow and confusion, I sought to connect with others who'd navigated big life disruptions. What began as a series of informal conversations eventually grew into a podcast called *A Slight Change of Plans*, which I started in 2021. Each episode was an opportunity to have a one-on-one conversation with someone who'd gone through a life-altering change: a young, self-proclaimed "health nut" who was diagnosed with aggressive bone cancer, a woman who found out that her late husband had had an affair, a friend of mine who'd lost her little sister in a car accident.

I didn't know what their stories might reveal, but I hoped that my academic expertise might lend me a unique perspective. In my work as a cognitive scientist, I've spent the past two decades exploring the human mind through disciplines like psychology, neuroscience, and philosophy. I've studied how we develop our beliefs, make decisions, and respond to uncertainty, risk, and failure. And so, in these interviews, I focused on understanding people's interior lives—what was shifting *within* them as they went through their changes. What were they experiencing on a psychological level that might not be visible to us from the outside?

I was moved by my guests' reflections and often thought back to what they'd shared with me. After spending more than a hundred hours interviewing people, I noticed patterns emerging across their stories. People whose situations looked nothing alike on the surface were nevertheless encountering similar challenges. For example, the cancer patient who felt like his body had failed him and the woman who was cheated on by her husband struggled with a similar feeling of betrayal. And it wasn't merely the challenges that people had in common; they were also using a shared set of strategies to overcome them. Those of us going through changes of all kinds are far more connected than we may have thought. We can learn from one another's stories, even when they don't look like our own. I was heartened by this realization, and also energized by it. There was so much to potentially discover about the universality of the change experience; it was clear that I'd only just scratched the surface. I wanted to combine long-form interviewing with our best understanding of how the mind works to build a deeper well of wisdom to draw from during life's toughest moments. And that's what led me to this book.

·

I've written this for anyone who is currently in the choppy waters of a change, is trying to make sense of a past change, or is anxious about a future change. This book is part narrative and part practical guide, rooted in the latest scientific research. I started this project by seeking out people with remarkable stories of change whom I'd never interviewed before. I then spoke with each of them repeatedly, over a period of several years. Their motivations, reactions, and reflections frequently ran counter to what I would have gleaned from the basic facts of their stories. I am grateful for their willingness to open up in such an unfiltered way. They offer an intimate view into the experience of upheaval.

When we imagine what it will be like to navigate an unexpected change and its aftermath, we tend to assume that we'll be the same person from beginning to end. Research shows that we greatly underestimate how much we'll change in the future, even though we fully acknowledge that we've changed considerably in the past. This bias is known as the *end of history illusion*, a term coined by the psychologist Dan Gilbert and his coauthors. "People, it seems, regard the present as a watershed moment at which they have finally become the person they will be for the rest of their lives," they write.

But we are constantly evolving, and a major disruption in our lives can accelerate this process. When a big change happens *to* us, it can lead to profound change *within* us. The unique stresses and demands of being thrust into a new reality can uncover unexpected—and sometimes astonishing—insights about ourselves and the world around us. These insights, coupled with the experience of the change itself, can transform us in extraordinary ways.

This is an empowering realization. When we're daunted at the outset of a change, there is some comfort in knowing that the person who will undergo the full experience will be different from the person we are in this very moment. We will become new people on the other side of change, in ways we are capable of shaping. And so the relevant question isn't "How will I navigate this change?" but rather "How will I—with potentially new capabilities, values, and perspectives—navigate this change?"

The first half of this book tells the stories of people who, as they confront new circumstances, must grapple with all that they've lost. In their own way, they each experience an internal transformation that allows them to imagine freeing possibilities for themselves. The second half of the book shows how that sense of possibility can ripple outward and influence how we relate to others and the world. Together, these stories offer a portrait of our varied, complicated reactions to change and how we can learn to open ourselves up to it. I've been inspired to consider the changes in my own life through a new lens, a personal evolution that I share throughout the book.

A negative change can feel like an apocalypse, as if the world we knew has now been destroyed. But *apocalypse* comes from the Greek word *apokalypsis*, which actually means revelation. This etymology is instructive: change can upend us, but it can also reveal things to us. What if we saw the hardest moments in our lives as a chance to reimagine ourselves, rather than as something to just endure? What potential could change unlock within us? In going on this journey with others, I've become far more curious about who I can be on the other side of change. I hope that after reading this book, you'll come to feel the same way.

The Other
Side of Change

1

Locked In

On a warm October afternoon in 2018, Olivia Lewis wrapped up an assignment and walked from the campus library to her bike. A month earlier, she'd started her senior year at Virginia Commonwealth University with a clear resolution: to stop making such a big deal about her health issues. For nearly a decade, she'd been periodically plagued by a strange constellation of symptoms, including vision problems, facial numbness, dizziness, and crushing migraines. She was a regular at the doctor's office, but more often than not her symptoms would resolve while she waited for her appointment to begin, and the doctor would tell her that there was nothing actually wrong with her. Her friends, too, had grown impatient with her over the years; sometimes she noticed them sigh or roll their eyes when she told them of yet another headache. She hated the idea that her anxieties about her health might be taking a toll on her relationships. She told herself she would just have to toughen up.

But as she bent down to unlock her bike from the rack, she felt a sharp twinge in her neck. When she stood up, little gray and black specks appeared in her field of vision. A dull headache set in. She shook her head and got on her bike to go grab some lunch. It was probably nothing.

That evening, though, at a friend's house, Olivia again felt strange. She'd just plopped down on the couch to watch *American Horror Story* when, as the show's moody theme song filled the room, her face went numb. She began to feel faint and nauseated. She excused herself and slowly made her way to the bathroom. When she looked in the mirror, she saw black splotches where her reflection should have been. She blinked hard, then splashed water on her face. She looked at the mirror again. The black splotches were still there. She cast her eyes around the room, but the splotches followed her gaze. Maybe she needed to take a few breaths and calm down. She knelt on the floor, leaned her forehead against the bathtub, and closed her eyes.

A few minutes later, she cautiously opened her eyes. She could now see her legs clearly. The splotches were gone. Relieved, she picked herself up and fixed her hair in the mirror. As she walked back to the living room to rejoin her friends, she was grateful that she wouldn't have to make a scene in front of them.

Olivia had only recently started to feel like her peers accepted her. Growing up, she'd attended a private school where she was surrounded by kids from wealthy families. Olivia's family was middle class—her parents had taken out loans and cobbled together the money to afford the tuition—and her background made her stand out. Her classmates made fun of her clothes and the things she liked.

They disparaged her modest home and her family's minivan, with its dents and missing hubcaps. In the fifth grade, Olivia was voted "ugliest girl" on a list that circulated in her school.

But in the past few years it seemed as if things were beginning to go her way. She had built a tight-knit circle of friends in college—just a week ago, she'd invited them over for a dinner party where they feasted on a big pot of spaghetti while sharing stories and laughing late into the night. She and her boyfriend from high school, Shawn, had maintained a long-distance relationship, and she was looking forward to visiting him in a few weeks. She was also on track to graduate with a degree in communications and planned to get a master's degree in copywriting. After so many years of feeling inadequate, Olivia could finally see an exciting future taking shape before her.

Later that evening, as she and her roommate drove back to their apartment, Olivia rolled down the window, took in some fresh air, and let the serenity of the night sky soothe her nerves. She reassured herself that she was fine. Now her focus was on getting to bed. She had an important class in the morning, and she had a habit of sleeping through her alarms. She took a quick shower and then performed her nightly ritual: setting six consecutive alarms on her phone starting at 8 a.m., spaced ten minutes apart.

It was just after four in the morning when an excruciating sensation coursed through Olivia's body. It ran from her spine into her head, jolting her awake and causing her to lurch upright. As her body seized up, she fell out of her bed, and her skull crashed directly onto the hardwood floor. Her head throbbed. She needed help.

She tried to reach for her phone, which was dangling off the side of her bed by its power cord, a mere inch above her face. But her arm wouldn't move. She tried to yell for her roommate. Her mouth wouldn't move, either. Suddenly, a cascade of fluids erupted from her body. A warm, thick substance oozed out of her ears. A puddle of urine formed beneath her. A mixture of vomit and blood bubbled up in her mouth. If she hadn't landed on her side, she thought, she might have choked on it. Though she was not particularly religious, she found herself talking to God: *Is this it? Am I just going to die like this?* She lay frozen in place for about two hours, fighting to keep herself awake. Then a strange sense of peace descended upon her. She allowed herself to drift into the darkness.

The next thing Olivia became aware of was the footsteps of her roommate, who'd burst into Olivia's room, annoyed by the incessant beeping of alarms. Olivia heard her roommate scream, "Oh my God!" The alarms continued to go off. *Beep. Beep. Beep.* Her roommate was now calling 911. Olivia registered all of this as if it were coming from far away. She could hear the wails of an ambulance siren. Soon, a medic was leaning over her, asking her questions. "Olivia! Olivia, can you hear me?"

When Olivia woke up, or sort of woke up—her eyes were still closed—she was lying flat in a bed and hooked up to a ventilator. The metronomic noises of hospital machines filled the air. Two people were talking. They sounded like her parents, and they sounded distressed. *Do they even know I'm alive in here?* Olivia thought, with sudden panic. *Are they going to pull the plug?* But, before she could do anything, she again drifted out of consciousness.

The next time she came to, her eyes opened. A nurse in blue scrubs was dabbing a wet sponge against Olivia's lips, while doctors talked to one another by the side of her hospital bed.

When she woke up again, a kind-looking woman she didn't know was strumming a guitar at her bedside, singing a song by Maroon 5, one of Olivia's favorite bands. When the woman finished the song, she asked Olivia if there was another one she might like to hear. Olivia heard the question, but the words passed over her like air.

And then, later, her aunt was sitting next to her, looking at her intently and holding up a board with each letter of the alphabet printed on it. *What were the letters for?* "Olivia," her aunt said. "Olivia, if you can understand what I am saying, please blink."

Olivia blinked.

•

Olivia had suffered a massive brain-stem stroke, which damaged the regions of her brain that control voluntary muscle movement for the entire body—except for the eyes. The stroke had left her with a condition called locked-in syndrome. Unable to voluntarily move, speak, make facial expressions, chew, or swallow, people with locked-in syndrome can mistakenly be thought to lack consciousness altogether. They do, however, retain their full cognitive abilities and personality traits; they are able to think, reason, and feel the same emotions as before. Their cardiovascular, digestive, urinary, and other autonomic systems also generally continue to function, though breathing support is often required. Some people with locked-in syndrome can make noises or vocalizations, like crying or laughing.

The condition gained greater recognition after the publication of the memoir *The Diving Bell and the Butterfly*, by Jean-Dominique Bauby, a former editor in chief of the French magazine *Elle*. Bauby suffered a brain-stem stroke in December 1995. After being in a coma for twenty days, he awoke in a hospital to find that he was unable to initiate any muscle movement, except for the muscles controlling his left eyelid, which allowed him to blink. To help him communicate, his speech therapist would recite the letters of the alphabet, and Bauby would blink when she arrived at the correct letter. Using this method, he could slowly spell out words, letter by letter. (In other cases, like Olivia's, caregivers will slide a finger along a board that lists the letters of the alphabet, and patients blink when they arrive at the correct letter.) Bauby completed his memoir this way, spending at least three hours a day on it for two months. He wrote about what it was like to grieve the loss of basic pleasures, such as hugging his son. The memoir's title offers a metaphor: his body is the diving bell, a rigid, heavy chamber that divers use to go deep into the ocean, and his mind is the butterfly, fluttering about but trapped within.

Locked-in syndrome is exceptionally rare; it's estimated that fewer than one thousand people in the United States currently have it. There is no cure, and, although some people are able to recover limited voluntary motor function after extensive rehabilitation, the long-term prognosis is very poor: the vast majority of patients never regain significant motor control. They continue to live with severe constraints, requiring round-the-clock care to meet their daily needs and to prevent complications that can result in death—Bauby himself died fifteen months after his diagnosis, from pneumonia.

Olivia did not know any of this as she drifted in and out of consciousness, her mind one big jumble from the steady stream of narcotics and other medications that were being pumped into her body through an IV. She didn't know that she was being kept alive entirely by machines, or that she'd had brain surgery days earlier. Nor did she know that the hospital chaplain had informed her mother that Olivia was, per the hospital's judgment, "past the point of reasonable return." Physicians were recommending that Olivia move into a nursing facility. Her grandmother, a school psychologist, was mentally preparing the family for Olivia's death. All Olivia knew was that she had to focus on blinking so that she could communicate her needs.

By the end of her first week in the hospital, Olivia gained more lucidity as doctors weaned her off some of the medications. She became consumed with figuring out what had happened to her. She painstakingly blinked out question after question. Her mom explained to her that she'd had a stroke, which had left her in a locked-in state. But Olivia was still unable to internalize that her body had been profoundly altered.

It was only when her boyfriend, Shawn, brought his family to visit the following week—his parents, aunt, and uncle filing into her cramped hospital room—that the gravity of her condition began to dawn on her. As Shawn and his family stood at the foot of her bed, trying to puncture the silence by sharing lighthearted memories from a summer beach trip they'd taken with Olivia, she sensed their unease.

Oh God, they must feel so awkward right now, Olivia thought. *Do something to make them feel more comfortable. Fix this.*

Olivia had always been intimidated by Shawn's family. They ran in different, more elite social circles than hers, frequenting the local country club and living in a wealthy part of town. Every time Olivia went over to Shawn's house for dinner, his dad made her feel as if she were being interviewed for a job she had no chance of getting. Convinced that she didn't have his family's approval because she wasn't accomplished enough or pretty enough or sophisticated enough, Olivia had joined them for their summer vacation to the beach, determined to win them over. In the weeks leading up to the trip, she brainstormed ways to show them that she was worthy of their son. Sure, she was currently working as a hostess at a restaurant, but it was her competitive fall internship at a marketing agency that she really cared about. Oh, and did she mention all the books she was reading? Despite her best attempts, though, she had left the trip knowing that it hadn't been enough. She would simply have to try harder next time.

But as Olivia lay in her hospital bed, she could of course do nothing. With a tracheotomy tube now hanging from her neck and no ability to make facial expressions, she could not project poise and grace. She could not thank Shawn's family for coming or encourage their halting efforts to connect with her. She could not make jokes about the hospital food or nod along and offer reassurance that she knew they meant well—that their nervous laughter and tense body language were *totally* fine, *totally* understandable.

As Shawn's family got ready to leave Olivia's room, his uncle walked over to her bedside. He hesitated for a moment, uncertain about how exactly he ought to say goodbye. He placed his hand gently on hers. "Hang in there, Olivia," he whispered kindly. Suddenly, the room filled with loud, piercing screams—*like a hyena's*, Olivia thought. Then it hit her. *She* was the one making the sounds. She was crying uncontrollably, but it was coming out as screeches. Alarmed that they might have said something wrong to cause Olivia's outburst, Shawn's family quickly ushered themselves out. This was more than Olivia could bear.

Afterward, when she was alone with Shawn, Olivia used her blinks to apologize for having made a scene. She wasn't sure why this particular moment had led her to break down. For nearly two weeks now, she'd endured the harrowing experience of being locked in. Why had it taken interacting with Shawn's family for the magnitude of it all to register? Why was she concerned with how she appeared to her boyfriend's family when she couldn't swallow a bite of food, use the bathroom, speak, or move a single limb on her own?

As the weeks passed, though, Olivia could not shake her self-consciousness—this deep, instinctual feeling that everyone else's opinion of her mattered so much, even more than her own suffering. She cried from embarrassment when nurses discussed her bowel movements in front of Shawn and her friends. She cried when her team of physicians shared every detail about her physical state with medical residents. She cried when one of her closest friends, Emily, brought her new boyfriend along on a visit, and Olivia—her mouth now hanging open by default due to the paralysis of her jaw and facial muscles—drooled on herself in front of them. Olivia cursed so loudly to herself that she wondered if Emily and her boyfriend could hear the words reverberating through her skull. That night, as was now the case every night, Olivia cried, her wails rousing patients nearby.

It had taken so long for Olivia to feel like other people were accepting her, and now she could no longer be who she wanted to be in front of them. Friends from high school and college came to visit, as did her professors, the dean of her college, and even her boss from her internship. Though she was grateful for the outpouring of care, Olivia resented their visits. She could not stand being so exposed. It was easier to just not see anyone.

At night, staring at the ceiling from her hospital bed, Olivia thought about evenings back in high school, when she'd complained about doing the dishes after dinner. She closed her eyes and conjured up the green-apple scent of the dish soap. She imagined herself standing in front of the sink, slowly and methodically washing each plate, bowl, and utensil by hand. Then she made a promise to the universe: *If I ever recover, I will never, ever complain about doing the dishes again.*

•

Olivia's initial physical-therapy sessions involved a relatively basic task: sitting upright. Her therapists would prop her up against a sturdy set of pillows in her hospital bed and challenge her to sit in this position for only a minute or two. But the sessions were excruciating, the pain in her limbs so fierce and unrelenting that she would sometimes vomit.

"I-D-O-N-T-W-A-N-T-T-O-B-E-H-E-R-E," she blinked repeatedly

to her parents. Why had this happened to her, of all people? She rarely drank, never did drugs, ate well, and exercised regularly. Every time a nurse came around with scissors or a needle, Olivia imagined lunging for the instrument and stabbing herself in the neck. She wondered if she might be able to persuade a friend to bring her pills so that she could overdose. The thought of having such agency was intoxicating.

Olivia's family knew that she was in desperate need of inspiration. Her grandfather, a former rehabilitation counselor, discovered the memoir *Running Free*, written by a woman named Kate Allatt, who had become locked in after suffering a stroke at the age of thirty-nine. Kate had made a miraculous recovery, regaining her ability to speak and walk in less than six months. She had even gone on to run in a race. As Olivia's grandfather read the memoir aloud, Olivia clung to the details of Kate's story. She decided that she, too, would have a miraculous recovery. If she didn't, she told herself, she would have no choice but to move someplace far away and live underground, maybe in a cave. She would cut off contact with everyone.

In the weeks that followed, Olivia became obsessed with Kate's recovery, memorizing every element of her rehabilitation plan. She asked her friends and family to email Kate on her behalf, requesting more detailed information about how and when exactly she had met certain milestones. Kate even became a bit of a hero among Olivia's friends. When they came to visit Olivia in the hospital, they'd scroll through Kate's Instagram account and show Olivia videos and photos to encourage her.

One afternoon, at Olivia's request, her grandfather opened YouTube and found a TEDx talk that Kate had given. He stationed his iPad in front of Olivia so that she could watch it with headphones, and then he returned to his chair to read a book. Because his You-Tube account was set to autoplay, though, a new video with similar content immediately started after Kate's finished. This one was about a woman who'd become locked in at the age of twenty and had only minimally recovered over the years. Olivia watched in horror as images of this woman's daily life played out on-screen, but she could not yell out to her grandfather to stop the video. As it played on, she grew increasingly panicked. Finally, the video ended, but the possibility of encountering another story like this one became her greatest source of anxiety. She asked her grandfather to watch the iPad carefully whenever he played things for her in the future so that she could shield herself from any stories that did not resemble Kate's. What she needed from her family was constant reassurance, often two or three times a day, that Kate's story would be her story.

But by December, two months after her stroke, it was clear that Olivia's recovery was not at all resembling Kate's. Other than regaining the ability to breathe on her own, Olivia felt she'd barely made any progress: she could only tilt her neck a tiny bit upward, raise her left arm by an inch or so, and sometimes lift her left index finger by a centimeter. When she'd first moved her finger, her family had cheered out loud. It was a remarkable achievement, and not one to be taken for granted, given the fates of so many other locked-in patients. But Olivia felt patronized. She was going to be the next Kate. Why couldn't her family understand this? Being able to *walk* would be a milestone worth celebrating.

Her grandfather tried to give Olivia more realistic expectations, telling her that she might experience a range of outcomes and that that was okay. They should rejoice in any improvement, however modest. But Olivia rejected this advice. The prospect of being a diminished version of herself was simply intolerable. How would anyone—her boyfriend, her friends, her community—accept her? How would she even accept herself? In order to go on, she denied the possibility of anything less than a full and speedy recovery.

Before her stroke, Olivia could not have imagined, even with her health-related anxieties, just how suddenly she'd be thrust into uncharted territory. The same can be true for any of us; in a moment, a change can disrupt all that was familiar. And though the changes we face may be nowhere near as severe as what Olivia experienced, they can still send shock waves through our lives. When a romantic relationship ends, we must conceive of a life without the other person. When we get laid off, we might be unable to pay our bills. When we receive a diagnosis of depression, we may struggle with the stigma that surrounds it.

As we muddle through these transitions, it can be tempting to deny our new situation as a way of protecting ourselves from negative emotions like grief, shame, fear, or helplessness. Although denial commonly occurs in the immediate aftermath of a change, it can also emerge later on, in different ways and at varying degrees of intensity.

"People are constantly seeking a way to comprehend what is happening to them," writes the psychologist Richard Lazarus. "This *ongoing process* of construing reality is a constantly changing one, depending on many variables within and outside of the person." Lazarus says that, when it comes to denial, "we are dealing with flux, and we must always be aware of the slippery nature of the event we are trying to understand."

Denial can take different forms. If a person is experiencing *first-order denial*, they will deny the basic facts of their situation, like the diagnosis they've received or the death of a loved one. If, like Olivia, they're experiencing *second-order denial*, they will accept the basic facts of their situation but deny the implications of those facts. They might minimize the seriousness of what is happening or project an overly optimistic view of the path ahead. They might also engage in avoidance and steer clear of anything that contradicts their narrative, as Olivia did when she shut out recovery stories that weren't like Kate's. You can think of denial as a kind of psychological immune response: the moment our minds detect a threat to our internal state, protective measures are deployed.

Olivia's denial was a response to a threat to her self-identity. In the months following her stroke, she held on to the belief that she would quickly recapture her old self, not just because she was in pain and wanted it to end, or because she wanted to walk, talk, and eat on her own, spend time with her friends and hug her boyfriend, and do the activities she loved—though, of course, all of this was true. On a deeper level, she experienced denial because her stroke had destroyed the version of her who was just starting to feel like she belonged. For any of us, our attachment to a specific identity can stand in the way of accepting our new reality. If you anchor your worth to your reputation as a parent, you might initially dismiss reports that your child is having behavioral problems in school. If you pride yourself on excelling at work, you might refuse to accept a poor performance review. If you've long valued your steadiness during stressful times, you might struggle to accept the onset of an anxiety disorder.

A threat to our sense of self is of course only one potential cause of denial. Denial can also stem from a fear that you, or those you love, lack the skills or resources to handle the consequences of a change. For example, a parent who receives a scary medical diagnosis might fool themselves into believing they're not actually sick so that they can avoid burdening their young children with the news. Denial can also emerge if your change carries a social stigma and you're afraid of how others might now treat you. As another example, when you're responsible for causing the change—perhaps your excess spending has led you into debt—you might engage in denial because it's easier to ignore your situation than to acknowledge the decisions you've made.

In certain contexts, denial can be beneficial. It can offer us a powerful feeling of control, motivation, and hope. "There is a grace in denial," write the grief researchers Elisabeth Kübler-Ross and David Kessler. "It is nature's way of letting in only as much as we can handle." One study explored the recovery trajectories of patients who had been hospitalized for heart problems. Those with high levels of denial had better short-term outcomes than those with low levels; high-denial patients spent less time in intensive care and had fewer heart-related symptoms during their hospital stays. For Olivia, her belief that her recovery would mirror Kate's not only boosted her optimism but provided a jolt of motivation to push her through a grueling physical-rehabilitation regimen.

But denial has its downsides. The same study on patients with heart problems showed that those with high levels of denial had worse outcomes in the year after their discharge from the hospital: compared with low-denial patients, they were less consistent in following their medical recommendations and ended up requiring more rehospitalization. For Olivia, the downside of her specific denial was that it set her up for potential devastation in the likely event that she never recovered as fully as Kate had.

As Olivia lay in her hospital bed, she decided that if she really wanted to get back to who she'd been at a rate that was acceptable, she would need a change of scenery. Her days had fallen into a rhythm, with her friends visiting her between their classes in the afternoon and Shawn occasionally spending the night on a pullout cot. She appreciated their support but also felt stuck. As she saw it, she was wasting her mental energy feeling anxious about her appearance and trying to make her interactions less awkward, when what she really needed to focus on was learning to walk again.

And so, when her family told her about an opportunity for treatment at one of the top rehab centers in the country—Spaulding Rehabilitation Hospital in Boston, more than five hundred miles away from her family's home in Virginia—Olivia didn't hesitate. Because she wouldn't have the ability to press an emergency call button or yell out if an issue arose, she would require round-the-clock care at Spaulding. Fortunately, her aunt and uncle already lived in Boston, and her grandfather offered to move there to spend his days with her. Olivia was thrilled. The change would spare her friends, and especially Shawn, the messiness of it all—her expressionless face, her physical pain, her hyena shrieks. She would work hard, away from their gaze, and when they came to visit she would be ready. *I will be back to my old self,* she thought.

•

"P-H-O-T-O-W-A-L-L," Olivia blinked. It was the third day in a row that she had pleaded with her aunt to decorate the walls of her new room at Spaulding with pictures from her pre-stroke life. Olivia obsessed over the photo wall. From morning to night, as she stared out her window at a bleak January sky, the same thought looped in her head: the photos needed to go up so that her new rehabilitation therapists in Boston would know Old Olivia—a construct that had recently taken shape in her mind—who was fun-loving, had a promising career, and hung out with artsy friends who had cool tattoos.

Olivia felt this was especially important because she'd been told that her new team of therapists would be close to her in age, not like the sixty-something caregivers she'd had in Virginia. If she was going to have her peers assisting her with her bedpan, Olivia reasoned, they should at least be made aware of who she *really* was. She tried again: "P-H-O-T-O." Her aunt, who had been sifting through a mountain of hospital paperwork, let out a deep sigh. Yes, she promised patiently, she'd put up the photos for Olivia at the end of the week.

That would be too late. The following morning, Olivia's care team—an occupational therapist, a speech therapist, and a physical therapist—came by her room to introduce themselves. *You have got to be kidding me,* Olivia thought when she saw their youthful faces. But her therapists didn't give her much time to dwell on her anxiety. They immediately got to work, running a series of tests and assembling a structured, aggressive rehabilitation regimen. In speech therapy, Olivia's first goal would be to raise her tongue to touch the roof of her mouth; in physical therapy, it would be to gain flexibility in her limbs, with the help of a therapist's gentle stretching.

Over the next few days, as her rehab schedule filled up, Olivia was struck by how her therapists didn't seem to care about the things she thought they would care about. She understood, of course, that they were unfazed partly because it was their job to be unfazed. But there was something so consistently nonchalant, so unpatronizing in how they interacted with her. Every time she began a rehab session, her physical therapist, Will, would have to lift her from her wheelchair and swing her over his shoulder before situating her in the therapy gym. Because her head faced the ground in this position and her mouth persistently hung open, she would inevitably drool on the floor, leading her to feel mortified. But Will would just wipe her mouth and the floor and then proceed with their session. Anytime her speech therapist, Esther, walked by Olivia's room and saw that Olivia had slid down her inclined hospital bed, she'd gently push her back to her original position, as though it were as ordinary as holding a door open for someone. One day, when the hospital staff had only an extra-large and puffy diaper for Olivia, she was even more self-conscious than usual, certain her therapists would notice the diaper through her pants. Like a hawk, she studied their gaze, awaiting their reaction when they first spotted it. But no reaction ever came—it just didn't seem to matter. Olivia started to relax.

Her hours of rehab with them, as exhausting as they were, stood in contrast to the increasingly awkward daily sessions she had with the hospital psychologist during her lunch hour. As her grandfather placed small spoonfuls of soft foods like applesauce and cheesecake on Olivia's tongue—and as she struggled to execute the arduous choreography of chewing and swallowing—the psychologist would stand in the middle of the room and observe her. Between Olivia's laborious swallows, the psychologist would pepper her with questions: "Do you find yourself missing your old life? How often do you feel negative thoughts about the future, Olivia? Do you feel sad?" Olivia found the questions preposterous, almost hilarious in their absurdity. But she was eager to earn a reputation as an easy patient and was already concerned that her frozen facial expression might make her appear rude. She earnestly blinked out answers using the letter board her grandfather was holding up: "V-E-R-Y-S-A-D."

On Valentine's Day, just over a month after Olivia's move to Boston, Shawn came to visit her at Spaulding for the first time. In recent weeks, she had detected fissures in their relationship. His texts were growing shorter and more formal, and they usually came only in response to the messages Olivia had sent him through her caregivers. She sensed that he secretly wanted to end their relationship but felt too guilty to go through with it. She had already lost so much; she couldn't afford to lose Shawn too. She knew the relationship was hanging by a thread, so she made every effort to keep that thread intact. She never complained to him about her physical pain. She never told him that she wished he'd check in on her more. She never shared with him that she feared he just didn't love her anymore. Instead, she asked her parents to send him care packages on her behalf.

That evening in the hospital, Shawn gave Olivia a little Valentine's gift: Goldfish crackers and Hershey's Kisses. These had long been her favorite snacks, but she was nowhere close to being able to eat them. Shawn's gift was a devastating reality check. Olivia had left for Boston with the goal of making exceptional progress, but here she was, still unable to chew on a cracker or nibble on a small piece of chocolate, still unable to vocalize a single word, still unable to give her boyfriend even a peck on the cheek. It was obvious Shawn had expected her to be much further along. In response to the gift, she simply blinked, "I-L-O-V-E-Y-O-U."

•

Though Olivia's improvements were accruing slowly relative to her expectations, she was in fact making *incredible* progress. Thanks largely to her therapists, she'd reached a major milestone: she was now capable of eating soft foods, which meant her feeding tube could be removed. This freed her up to do therapy at the rehab center's swimming pool, which would unlock a far wider range of exercises.

Olivia's occupational therapist, Nick, also came up with a new way for her to communicate that was less tedious than using the letter board. Since she was able to raise her left index finger by a centimeter— and could now also move her shoulder ever so slightly, enough to guide her hand in all four directions—she could try to tap on a smartphone. Nick created a special sling for her arm that hung from the ceiling, then placed her iPhone on a rubber pad, angled so that her finger could easily tap its keyboard. Each day, he had her use the phone to respond to the same question: What goal would she like to achieve today? At first, Olivia found the phone setup maddening. After hours spent trying to tap the correct letters, she was still producing gibberish. But she stuck with it, and soon she was able to type out coherent answers. One morning, Nick gave her the usual prompt. Olivia thought for a second and then slowly typed, "runnnnnoing a marthtgfon woulpd berr nice."

It was the first joke she'd made since her stroke. As Nick laughed, she realized just how good it felt to show this more irreverent side of herself. In the weeks that followed, she let her guard down more and more. One afternoon, when Will, her physical therapist, worked with Olivia to get her fitted for a power wheelchair that she could operate with her working index finger, she grew frustrated. Each of the wheelchairs she tried was too big for her small, weak frame. Despite all the pillows Will used to prop her up, she kept sliding off the seat. In the past, she would have gone out of her way to hide her negative emotions and project an easygoing, unflappable demeanor. But this time, as she unsuccessfully tried out a fourth wheelchair, she allowed herself to unravel in front of Will. Her wails filled the room. She blinked furiously at her grandfather, who held up the letter board and relayed her message to Will: Why was she learning how to use a wheelchair when she would one day walk again? The clock was ticking, and she was so far away from becoming Old Olivia.

Will, unruffled by her outburst, considered the question. "I don't know what's going to happen in the future," he gently replied. "We'll try our hardest to get you walking, but it's very important that we focus on today."

Olivia was too distraught to internalize Will's message in that moment, but as her emotions settled in the following weeks, she kept returning to his words. For the past several months, she'd revealed sides of herself that she had long been determined to hide, yet her team of therapists had accepted her. Reflecting on this left her with a radical idea: maybe *she* should accept who she was in this very moment. It was an enormous thought, too enormous for her to process at once.

The idea was still percolating when, that spring, a friend from college visited and brought Olivia's laptop with her. It was the first time since her stroke that Olivia had been reunited with her computer, and on a sunny day the next week, she used her working index finger to explore. Out of habit, she opened Spotify and scrolled through her old playlists. There it was—her guilty-pleasure playlist, chock-full of pop songs with catchy hooks from bands like The Fray and Maroon 5. She pressed play. As she lay in her bed, the songs instantly lifted her spirits. Her friends had made fun of her taste in music, and she was acutely aware that people passing by her room might hear these songs and judge her. But Olivia didn't care; she wasn't trying to impress anyone. She turned up the volume and danced along in her head.

One April evening a few weeks later, Olivia was in the therapy gym, clocking some after-hours rehab on a specialized bike that used electrical pulses to initiate rotations in her legs. Her time in residence at Spaulding was coming to an end because her insurance coverage was running out. She was sad to be leaving; she'd grown close to her team of therapists in the months they'd spent together. Before heading out each evening, Will, Esther, and Nick had made a point of stopping by Olivia's room to say good night, occasionally teasing her for once again ordering guacamole and sofritas from Chipotle for dinner. Sometimes they texted her after work, to check in or to share a funny anecdote. And they let her into their lives, too. Olivia had formed an especially close bond with Esther. They connected on refreshingly ordinary topics, like Olivia's days playing field hockey and her relationship with Shawn. Esther reciprocated with stories of her own—about a guy she used to date, and her experience playing sports in college. *I'm not just their job*, Olivia realized. *They seem to genuinely like me.*

As the bike facilitated leg rotation after leg rotation, Olivia saw Nick out of the corner of her eye finishing up a session with another patient. Earlier in the day, Olivia had met with her full care team to discuss what her post-discharge rehab plan could look like. When Nick was done, he came over to ask her about her thoughts on the meeting. She had been frustrated by some aspects of the discussion and began typing a response on her phone. Tap. Tap. As she typed, Olivia noticed that she was drooling on herself. Her instinct in these situations was to take advantage of the fact that she could tilt her neck slightly upward to minimize her drool and, in turn, her embarrassment.

But this time Olivia didn't tilt her head. She remained focused on her phone screen. Tap. Tap. Tap. Saliva dribbled down Olivia's chin and onto her shirt, but she continued typing. Nick went to fetch a washcloth. *You know what? I don't care,* she thought. *What matters is what I want to say to him. This is who I am right now.*

It dawned on Olivia that she'd been trying to win other people's approval not just since she'd landed in the hospital but for as long as she could remember. "It honestly makes me nauseous now, but looking put together and being seen as 'going places'—all of this stuff felt essential to my having value," Olivia said. Since childhood, she'd learned to try to present a version of herself that she believed would fit in. She resolved not to complain about her health concerns, because of what other people might think. She regularly downplayed her own discomfort to make those around her feel more comfortable. Even her relationship with Shawn, she realized, was largely motivated by her desire for approval. "Because I felt I wasn't likable enough or accomplished enough on my own," she said, "I'd thought that having this amazing person as a boyfriend would help me belong more. A huge part of my identity was that I had been *picked* by this person."

Even if our self-identity is not as tethered to external validation as Olivia's once was, each of us has an identity that is *contingent*: it might depend, for example, on some combination of the roles you play, the activities or jobs you do, or the communities to which you belong. There are of course benefits to rooting your identity in these kinds of sources. Defining yourself as an athlete, for instance, can bring structure and meaning to your everyday life and foster a sense of camaraderie with fellow athletes. But anchoring your identity too strongly to any given thing also carries risks: when a change threatens that very thing, it can be destabilizing and cause you to enter a state of denial. The stakes simply feel too high.

At Spaulding, Olivia considered what it might be like to rely less on others for validation. What if she started trusting herself more and establishing her values and goals on her own terms? As she entertained this new way of seeing herself, the threat her condition posed to her self-identity diminished. She had put so much pressure on herself to make a fast recovery, but perhaps there was no real timeline after all. "I still wanted to recover quickly, of course," she said. "But I had this new sense that it was now going to be *my* timeline, not the one I had set to prevent my boyfriend from breaking up with me or to ensure my friends didn't leave me behind."

In early May 2019, seven months after her stroke, Olivia was set to be discharged from Spaulding. She would have to rely on outpatient therapy and her own tenacity from here on out. But, despite the immense recovery challenges and the uncertainty that lay ahead, she actually felt okay, buoyed by her ability to now prioritize what was actually important: "If I was constantly worried about my head being in a certain position so that I didn't drool in front of people," she said, "was I really focused on what I needed to accomplish in therapy that day?"

On the afternoon of her discharge, Will, Esther, and Nick threw Olivia a goodbye party, complete with Shake Shack burgers cut up into tiny pieces that Olivia could now chew and swallow. As they all sat around a table in the common area, they made jokes and engaged in playful banter, with Olivia typing out her thoughts with her phone. "Before the stroke, I was always intent on matching the energy of the room around me—to act happy or laugh along, even when I didn't think something was funny," she said. This time, however, her joy was authentic. "Even though I had so much weighing on my mind about my future, I was just genuinely happy in that moment." Back when she was in Virginia, she could never have imagined hanging out with her peers and feeling so utterly unencumbered, so comfortable not trying to act in any particular way.

And so, when Shawn broke up with Olivia a few months later, she was amazed to discover that, while she was heartbroken, she was not destroyed. "I was committed to finding my way forward, for myself," she said. She deleted her social media accounts, so as not to compare her life with anyone else's. She downloaded audiobooks and music to keep her company during her daily grind of physical therapy. And, finally, she took out her phone and pulled up photos of Old Olivia. One by one, she deleted them all.

Denying our new reality is a common and understandable reaction to a negative change. It's natural to want to protect ourselves from painful emotions and to hold on to who we once were. Olivia engaged in denial because gaining other people's approval was central to her identity, and she feared that she couldn't get that approval in her new state. It was only when she began to reconceive of her identity and place less importance on people's opinions of her that her new state became less threatening. This allowed her to finally acknowledge the reality that her recovery would likely be complicated and incomplete.

As you think about navigating a change, you might consider whether your own identity is too firmly anchored to something relatively precarious, like your physical abilities, your mental acuity, or other people's perceptions of you. Or perhaps it's attached to something you ultimately lack full control over, like how exactly your children turn out or whether you get hired for a certain job. Are there ways that you can reimagine your identity so that it is more robust or nimble when life makes other plans for you?

You can also use an approach called *self-affirmation* to build your resilience during these challenging moments. Self-affirmation involves actively shifting your mental spotlight toward aspects of yourself that you value, but that, critically, are not threatened by the change you are going through. For instance, if you're navigating the end of a relationship, you might affirm that you value your creativity, or your spiritual life, or your role at work. Research shows that self-affirmation can make you less susceptible to denial because it reminds you that your identity does not hinge entirely on what's been affected or taken away by the change. In doing so, it reduces the perceived intensity of the threat, enabling you to more openly embrace your reality. In one study, researchers gave young women who were heavy alcohol consumers a pamphlet explaining that drinking too much could increase their risk of breast cancer. Some of these women were asked, prior to reading the pamphlet, to complete a self-affirmation exercise in which they wrote about something they highly valued in themselves that did not relate to their health. Those women who completed this exercise were more likely to be convinced by the pamphlet that they were in fact at a greater risk of cancer and were also more likely to declare an intention to drink less alcohol.

Spending years in conversation with Olivia has inspired me to revisit my own relationship with my identity and how I might make it more durable in the face of change. When I was a little kid, I dreamed of becoming a concert violinist. I was accepted into the Juilliard School's precollege program when I was nine. Every Saturday, my mom and I would get up at four-thirty in the morning and take a train from Connecticut to New York City for a full day of classes. Within a few years, I began winning concerto competitions and soloing with orchestras, and the renowned violinist Itzhak Perlman invited me to be his private student.

There was so much I loved about the violin. I loved emotionally connecting with others through my music. I relished the feeling of mastering a challenging passage and the creativity involved in shaping a phrase. I also felt a sense of belonging within my musical community. I was often bullied by the girls in my neighborhood. I knew that I looked different—I was one of a few brown kids in a predominantly white school—and I internalized their cruelty as evidence that I was deeply flawed in some way. By contrast, my friends at Juilliard, many of whom had moved to New York City from all over the world, embraced me.

Everything was going according to plan until, at age fifteen, I overstretched my pinkie playing a technically challenging piece by

Paganini and damaged tendons in my hand. After the doctor did his examination, he told me to take an extended break so that the injury could heal. But my hand never got better, even with rest. I resumed playing on and off for over a year, but despite extensive physical therapy, cortisone injections, and anti-inflammatories, the pain never let up. Doctors eventually suggested that I give up the violin altogether. I rejected their advice. In giving up the violin, I wouldn't just be losing what I loved—I'd be losing *who I was*. I was in denial, desperately clinging to my old self and continuing to play and perform through pain. Finally, after an unsuccessful surgery, doctors told me in more definitive terms that my dream was over.

Since giving up the violin, I've had to make other career and life pivots, and each one was disorienting. Every time I took on a new pursuit, I once again anchored my value to it, precisely as I had done with the violin. When my circumstances inevitably changed and I could no longer do that thing, I became unmoored.

But what if, like Olivia, I could reconceptualize my identity? Although it was true that I could no longer play the violin, I hadn't lost what led me to love it in the first place. I revisited what those aspects were through the lens of self-identity: *I am a person who loves emotionally connecting with others, improving at a craft, being creative, and being part of a community.* It was only a matter of finding new outlets through which to express these parts of myself. For example, I've been able to satisfy my desire for connection through my role as an interviewer, and my passion for honing a craft in my work as a cognitive scientist. Moving forward, I'm slowly learning to attach my identity not just to specific pursuits, but to the underlying *features* of those pursuits that make me light up—in other words, to define myself not simply by *what* I do but by *why* I do it. It's a way to give myself a softer landing the next time my "what" is put at risk; my "why" will still be there, and it can help steer me toward my next chapter.

·

Olivia left Spaulding with a newfound sense of freedom about the road ahead. After each day of intensive outpatient therapy, she would return home to the bare-bones, temporary apartment in Boston she'd moved into with her aunt, uncle, and grandfather. She would continue her exercises with a singular focus for hours on end, and her hard work paid off: within a few months, she was making faster progress than ever before. She began moving around the apartment with the assistance of a walker that her grandfather helped stabilize. And she occasionally produced words that were intelligible, like "hi" and "water." The first sentence she uttered to her mom was "I love you."

Today, Olivia is back in Virginia, where she lives with her parents in her childhood home. Her recovery has been astonishing. She is able to do most things independently. Having regained most of her motor control, she can now walk with a wobbly gait and a limp. She can also speak clearly, but with a shaky voice that tires easily because her mouth remains partially paralyzed. And she is able to eat most foods, including, notably, Goldfish crackers and Hershey's Kisses. Doctors are still unsure what caused her stroke in 2018, but she takes medication daily to try to prevent blood clots.

Olivia first reached out to me through a message on Instagram. She had listened to my podcast, *A Slight Change of Plans*, and was eager to connect. I was taken by the warmth of her message, and I replied to her immediately. Within an hour, we were chatting on the phone. From the start of our conversations, Olivia was committed to guiding me through the nuances of her experience, eager to unpack each psychological shift that had unfolded within her along the way. Often, we'd look at the time and notice that hours had passed. Impressed by her vocal endurance, she'd joke that our chat should count as her speech-therapy requirement for the day.

Olivia is no longer invested in achieving a complete recovery. As time has passed, she's developed a greater capacity to accept her current physical state, whatever it may be. Recently, she did something she never would have let herself do in the early years following her stroke: she took an entire month off from physical therapy, using the time instead for reading, going on trips, and hanging out with friends. During one of our conversations, I noticed that Olivia couldn't stop smiling. As it turned out, while she was shopping for groceries the previous evening, she had decided that she was ready to date again. She said she was tired of letting arbitrary goals—like being allowed to drive, or regaining full control of her mouth so that her grin wouldn't be lopsided and kissing wouldn't be weird—hold her back. "I've come to the conclusion that there's never going to be a 'right' time for anything," she said. "If I make additional physical improvements, that's great. But every time I've reached a new milestone, I've known full well that it might be as far as I get. And so, I'm choosing to be happy with who I am at any given moment and to not put my life and my dreams on hold."

Embracing New Olivia, and actually *liking* this version of herself more than Old Olivia, has been a process. Over the years, she's found that being more open and assertive about her wants, needs, and anxieties has only deepened her relationships, not undone them. One of her greatest joys today is her bond with her mom, whom she now considers her best friend. And Olivia has switched career paths. Though she completed her bachelor's degree in communications in 2022, she is currently in graduate school to become a mental-health and physical-rehabilitation counselor.

Olivia has had a few frightening health episodes since returning home to Virginia, like when she experienced a mini stroke (fortunately, there was no lasting damage) and when she was hospitalized for extreme dizziness and other strange symptoms. There are plenty of days when she is frustrated, either because of her body's challenges or because she sees her friends, who are also in their late twenties, hitting life milestones—like getting married or having babies—that still seem far off for her. Nevertheless, she is grateful. "It took my getting stripped of everything to realize I was disappointed in who I was becoming, and I saw this as my chance to start over," she said. "It can take decades for people to reach the self-assured place I'm in. My stroke forced me to get there so much sooner than I would've otherwise, assuming I ever got there at all."

After her parents leave for work in the morning, Olivia sometimes goes into the kitchen, puts on music, and stands at the sink. She considers the light coming through the window and the sight of the trees outside. And then she does the dishes. As she washes them one by one, she takes a moment to enjoy the warm water running over her hands and the green-apple scent of the dish soap. "And I remind myself that I'm here," she said. "I've come this far."

2

Possible Selves

Dwayne Betts marked each passing day by etching a small vertical line onto the wall of his jail cell. He'd been here for seven nights so far. He hadn't been allowed to shower or change his clothes, nor had he been given a mattress or a pillow. On the first night, he'd taken off his sweater and laid it atop the concrete bed, hoping it would provide his scrawny, 126-pound body with some cushion and warmth. But the biting cold of winter was severe, and he struggled to sleep. To make matters worse, his cell was in the basement, and the absence of windows made it impossible to see the days come and go. His only connections to the outside world were the rare phone call and the sound of intermittent screams from men in nearby cells.

Dwayne had been charged with carjacking, robbery, and the use of a firearm in the commission of a felony. Just a month after his sixteenth birthday, he'd hopped into a car with a friend and three other guys he barely knew and headed to a shopping mall. Up until that point, Dwayne had lived just outside the violence of his friends in the neighborhood. He simply wasn't the type to fight. But on this particular evening he decided to ask the driver for a gun. The pistol would allow him to imagine himself as more than a coward.

Walking around the mall's parking lot, Dwayne and his friend came upon a man sleeping in his car. Dwayne tapped on the window with the tip of the gun and threatened the man, who got out of the car and gave up his wallet and keys. Dwayne and his friend then drove away with the car. The police caught up with them the following afternoon, on December 8, 1996.

Authorities had initially placed Dwayne in a juvenile detention center, but because his case involved a carjacking it was soon redirected to an adult criminal court. He faced the possibility of life plus thirteen years in prison. After pleading guilty to all charges, he was relocated to the county jail to await his sentencing hearing—and it was here that he started marking time on the walls. How long would it be, he wondered, before the lines he was marking lost their meaning? How long would it be before he stopped marking time altogether?

A few weeks later, Dwayne awoke to the sound of an officer walking by his cell door and dropping a piece of mail through the bars. The envelope bore his state number, 91580, which was now also a fixture on his right wrist, printed on a band he was required to wear at all times. He'd shared the number with his mom so that she could send him mail, but she still made it a point to write out his full name— Reginald Dwayne Betts—at the top of every envelope she sent him.

This letter was not from his mom, though. It was from a high school friend who was writing about a recent class trip and how much fun the day had been. Dwayne knew from the tone of the letter that his friend was not trying to rub anything in; he was just eager to maintain a connection with Dwayne. But it was too much. Dwayne set the letter down, then punched the wall of his cell.

On the day of his sentencing, Dwayne sat at the defendant's table and avoided eye contact with his family. His mother was seated a few rows behind him. She had planned to testify as a character witness but had come down with bronchitis and wouldn't be able to speak. Dwayne believed the real reason she'd lost her voice was a broken heart. Despite the severity of his charges, he was hopeful that the judge would give him a lighter sentence. "I still had metal braces connected by colorful rubber bands on my teeth," he said. "How could they not give me a second chance?"

Dwayne had always imagined that he would break free from his life in Suitland, Maryland, where he and his mom lived, and where he navigated the everyday realities of poverty and violence. When Dwayne was in the second grade, a teacher had told him that he was gifted, and he clung to that identity. Every Friday, he and his classmates were given the challenge of solving a hundred math problems before the period bell rang, and Dwayne took great pride in being able to complete every single one. When he was in middle school, while some of his friends in the neighborhood were out dealing drugs, he was being bused to and from a magnet school. And in high school, he was an honor student who was voted class treasurer, a position he'd run for so that he could bulk up his résumé in time for college admissions and fulfill his dream of studying engineering at Georgia Tech. And yet he'd risked it all to try to impress a few guys he hardly knew.

When the judge announced that Dwayne's sentence would be nine years in adult prison, his aunt let out a howl. As Dwayne was ushered back to his cell in handcuffs, he looked over to his family and friends and instinctively yelled out that he was going to be all right.

But he didn't believe his own words. He was not at all sure that he'd be okay. As soon as he was transferred from the county jail to prison, he was suffocated by terror. "The men around me—they were older and bigger than me. I was frightened by them because they were men and I was a kid," Dwayne said. The conversations he overheard among his fellow inmates were about what made them tough, never about what they feared. And though every minute of every day was regimented—from breakfast to yard time to the twice-daily prisoner counts—fights broke out frequently. Dwayne had little knowledge of the social hierarchy, or of what alliances existed. The prison nurse had even cautioned him against accepting anything from the other men.

Dwayne tried to make himself inconspicuous, avoiding eye contact and any unnecessary conversation. He adopted a permanent scowl that resembled those of the men around him. He knew he did not have the strength to protect himself if someone tried to hurt him. What would he do if somebody rushed into his cell? Would he fight them? Could he secure a knife somehow? Rumors swirled about the terrible things that had happened to the younger boys. There was a boy in a nearby cell even younger than Dwayne—he seemed to be about fourteen—named Jamil, and word was that someone had tried to rape him.

At night, in the safety of his cell, Dwayne's mind drifted to everything he was missing out on: dribbling his basketball on his walks to the library, talking on the phone with the girl he had a crush on, helping his mom shovel snow outside their home and fetching her a glass of water in the middle of the night. He conjured up the alternative future he could have experienced—finishing high school, attending Georgia Tech, making new friends, maybe having his first girlfriend. Some of these experiences weren't things he could catch up on later. He would never attend homecoming or prom. He would never graduate alongside his friends. His mom would never drop him off at his freshman dorm for college. His prison sentence had erased it all.

Dwayne's existence grew small, and not just because of the physical constraints of his cell. "There was no cultural reference, no narrative reference, no film reference of what I might be that would have allowed me to sleep at night. Who you gonna be at sixteen—Malcolm X?" he said. "If you're Black in America and go to prison, in one moment, with one guilty plea, the list of possibilities has been reduced to no possibilities."

That Dwayne had brought this upon himself made him feel ashamed and angry. As he contemplated his nine-year sentence, he was filled with dread. Now that he was a prisoner, was he going to develop a gambling habit and then get stabbed because he owed someone money? Was he going to start smoking and become addicted and then have to borrow money to get cigarettes? "It wasn't just the fear of violence I felt," he said. "It was the fear of everything that I might become."

One afternoon, a little over a year into his sentence, Dwayne was walking down a hallway when he was stopped by another prisoner. He was struck by the man's appearance. For months now, Dwayne had been doing his best to look as unkempt as possible—he'd stopped cutting his hair and shaving—in an effort to deflect attention. But the prisoner in front of him, a short, brown-skinned guy with a sturdy neck and the build of a boxer, had made a conscious choice to stand out. His prison clothes were crisply ironed. He had on a fresh pair of boots. His face was impeccably clean-shaven, his Afro well maintained. "He carried himself in such a dignified way, like a person in uniform," Dwayne said.

The man's name was Bilal. He offered Dwayne a warm smile and then said that he'd heard the rumors about someone trying to rape a teenager named Jamil. Bilal said he was eager to help Jamil and asked if Dwayne knew any details. Dwayne mumbled a noncommittal response. He was wary of talking to other inmates. Everyone in prison seemed to be out for themselves, and getting entangled in gossip could carry serious consequences. Plus, Bilal's questions about Jamil made him uneasy. Was Bilal a predator himself? Did he have an ulterior motive? Why was he so interested in Jamil?

But a few days later, out in the prison yard, Dwayne saw Bilal again. This time, Bilal was teaching Jamil and a handful of other young men how to box. Watching Jamil practice a punch, Dwayne connected the dots: Bilal was giving these young men a way to protect themselves. Dwayne felt something shift within him. He had interacted with Jamil a few times, and as far as he was concerned, Jamil was kind of an asshole. And yet Bilal had taken him under his wing anyway. In the weeks that followed, Bilal continued to give boxing lessons to Jamil and the other young men.

Dwayne regarded these lessons as a remarkable act of generosity. In choosing to protect others, Bilal defied the norms of ruthless self-interest that Dwayne had believed were necessary for survival behind bars. "He had this honorable willingness to go to bat for someone he didn't even know—to stand at the scratch line for them—in a place where vulnerability got you ruined," Dwayne said.

It occurred to Dwayne that even in the brutal conditions of prison, you could still choose to carry yourself in a certain way, to embody a set of values. "Prison is so structured and so regimented—wake up at this time, stand for count—that you come to hate all regimen," he said. "But Bilal was the kind of guy who woke up ahead of time, did two hundred and fifty push-ups, and stood at the door for count because he wanted everyone to know that he was always ready an hour *before* the guards ever came through the door." Bilal expanded Dwayne's understanding of what it could mean to be a prisoner. "How he dressed, how he carried himself, his care for young people even when allegiances in prison could get you killed—he was making this choice to say 'This is my identity.'" Dwayne saw for the first time that maybe he wasn't destined to become a certain type of person just because he was in prison. Perhaps there were other futures available to him.

·

Imagine receiving a magic photo album filled with pictures of yourself from a variety of possible futures. As you flip through the book, you see different snapshots of who you might become. On one page, you see pictures of yourself with a big family in a house in the suburbs. On another, you're living out of a suitcase, traveling the world. On other pages, you're battling a chronic illness or stuck in a dysfunctional relationship. Some of these pages might fill you with optimism, whereas others might evoke fear or sadness. Still others might simply surprise you, as you see versions of yourself, both good and bad, that you had never before contemplated.

As we go about our lives, we regularly conjure up these *possible selves*. When a college student daydreams about becoming a biologist—picturing herself in a lab coat, writing research papers, and giving talks—she is creating a possible self. When a star soccer player gets injured and tries to imagine a future without the sport, he is creating a possible self. When Dwayne worried that his prison sentence would condemn him to a future of violence and addiction, he, too, was creating a possible self. The concept of possible selves was introduced by the psychologists Hazel Rose Markus and Paula Nurius. These selves come in a number of forms: *hoped-for* selves reflect our aspirations, *feared* selves embody our worries, and *expected* selves represent our predictions about what we think is most likely to happen.

As we navigate a change, our set of possible selves can shift dramatically in response to our new circumstances, but sometimes our minds constrain us beyond what is necessary. Shaped by our prior experiences and our social and cultural environments, the possible selves we generate do not always encompass the full range of what is actually available to us. For example, we might carry unfounded assumptions or stereotypes about what possible selves exist for someone who drops out of school, or is a teen parent, or is incarcerated. These assumptions restrict our imagination about who we can be on the other side of change. In the same way that Olivia was unable to envision a happy life for herself if she never made a full recovery, Dwayne struggled to conceive of a promising future now that he was a prisoner.

And so, when change strikes, it can feel like our future has been determined, with certain possible selves now closed off to us. A person who becomes a caregiver for their partner might grieve the potential versions of themselves that now seem inaccessible; perhaps the new demands on their time make it harder to take up hobbies or to attend night school. In other cases, new possible selves that we never previously imagined now seem probable, if not inevitable—doors we never wanted to see open are now ajar. Like Dwayne, we may fear who we might become. Consider Nora McInerny, a writer and the host of the podcast *Terrible, Thanks for Asking*, who railed against her impending label of "widow" when her husband was diagnosed with terminal brain cancer at the age of thirty-five. Nora had a mental image of what it meant to be a widow that was based on the people she knew and the depictions she'd seen in popular culture. As she understood it, being a widow meant being defined by tragedy, perpetual sadness, and constant pity from others. "I did not want that," she said. "I did *not* want to be a dead-husband person."

·

A few weeks after meeting Bilal, Dwayne was disciplined for trying to prevent a guard from closing his cell door. He was sentenced to three months in solitary confinement in a tiny, dilapidated cell. The cell's window had no screen, and Dwayne had to use a garbage bag to try to seal it off; rain and insects still came in. He was allowed to leave his cell once every three days for a shower and twice a week for recreation. But recreation, which took place in an outdoor cage that "looked like a man-sized dog kennel," was terrifying. Men were released into the cage two at a time, and the cage was then locked. Dwayne soon stopped going out for recreation altogether.

Still, solitary confinement was a welcome reprieve from his regular prison life. Although it was stifling to be alone with his thoughts, he felt a kind of peace now that he was sequestered and protected from the threat of violence. He began writing letters to Bilal. It was Bilal who, in his distinctly tidy penmanship, had first reached out to Dwayne after Dwayne was moved to solitary. That he had chosen to write at all and take on a mentorship role moved Dwayne. "More than a man, Bilal represented an *idea* to me," Dwayne said. "Of what it means to be lovely."

Books were deemed contraband in solitary confinement, and Dwayne's books had been seized from him upon arrival. One day, though, he heard a call from a neighboring cell: "Yo, send me a book!" Seconds later, he heard a distinct sound as a book slid across the concrete floor from under one cell door to another. This sound repeated throughout the day—paperbacks made a particular ruckus, like birds flapping their wings. Dwayne discovered that his fellow prisoners were running a vibrant underground library. Inmates in regular prison had found a way to send books to those in solitary. They'd used torn-up bedsheets to create a forty-foot rope that hung like a laundry line between their respective prison buildings. The inmates would routinely fill pillowcases with books and inch them along the line to reach those in solitary.

Dwayne was initially scared to request a book for himself. He had long internalized the idea that it was too risky to ask the men around him for anything. But on one especially lonely night, Dwayne built up the courage to make his first request. He shouted out for a book. Moments later, a *Reader's Digest* anthology slid under his door. He read it in a single sitting. From that day forward, he read a new book every day.

Two days before his eighteenth birthday, having just finished a fantasy novel by R. A. Salvatore, Dwayne called out for another book. Soon came the familiar sound, followed by a thick volume that barely fit under his cell door called *The Black Poets*. The book appeared to be brand new, its pages still crisp. Dwayne had never heard of it. He studied the cover: bright white with an image of four colorful birds, their wings constrained by chains.

The book was a poetry anthology, first published in 1971 and edited by a poet and professor named Dudley Randall. Randall explained in the introduction that his aim was to present "the full range of black American poetry, from the slave songs to the present day." Folk poems and spirituals filled its pages, as well as works by Claude McKay, Langston Hughes, and Lucille Clifton. "The first literary black poets tried to write as whites for a white audience," Randall wrote. But, eventually, they turned to other sources for inspiration, like jazz and folk songs. This, Randall noted, had "freed black poets to create a new poetry."

Dwayne started at the beginning. He read poems by Robert Hayden, Margaret Walker, and Gwendolyn Brooks, all of which were new to him. Other than a Langston Hughes poem he'd been required to memorize and recite in grade school, Dwayne had never read poetry before. But he found the poems to be beautiful, even if he felt some remove from the experiences they depicted.

Just over halfway through the book, Dwayne came across a poem titled "For Freckle-Faced Gerald," by the Mississippi-born poet Etheridge Knight. It told the story of a young inmate who had been raped in prison:

> *Take Gerald. Sixteen years hadn't even done*
> *a good job on his voice. He didn't even know*
> *how to talk tough, or how to hide the glow*

of life before he was thrown in as "pigmeat"
for the buzzards to eat.

Dwayne sensed that Knight was writing from personal experience, from something he had witnessed up close. Knight described the precarity of life behind bars:

(No safety in numbers, like back on the block:
two's aplenty. three? definitely not.
four? "you're all muslims."
five? "you were planning a race riot."
plus, Gerald could never quite win
with his precise speech and innocent grin
the trust and fists of the young black cats.)

Reading the poem, Dwayne had a thought: *Freckle-faced Gerald didn't have a Bilal to protect him. But,* Dwayne realized, *Knight had played a version of Bilal.* So many people who'd endured the horrors of prison didn't have the chance to share or make sense of what they had been through. With "For Freckle-Faced Gerald," Knight proved that you could be a witness on their behalf and use words to record and dignify their experiences. As Dwayne saw it, Knight was standing at the scratch line for Gerald.

Bilal had shown Dwayne a landscape of possibility. Now Knight helped Dwayne pinpoint where on that landscape he could try to place himself. "I couldn't do what Bilal could do for Jamil, for anybody," Dwayne said. "I knew that wasn't my lane. But I could do what Knight did for the guys he wrote about." Knowing he would eventually have to send *The Black Poets* back into rotation in the underground library, Dwayne copied by hand the poems he most liked, including the ones by Knight. As he did so, a new possible self formed within him. "Etheridge Knight weaved prison's hurt into poetry, and for the first time I wanted to write a poem that wasn't for women," Dwayne would later write. "A poem that was for the dudes around me, carrying time like the heaviest albatross around their necks."

•

After reading Knight's work, Dwayne was profoundly altered. It was similar to what he'd felt when he first saw how Bilal carried himself in prison, and how he cared for the younger inmates. Observing Bilal's example gave Dwayne a new way of thinking about his circumstances, and about himself. "In prison, part of you is certain that the space you live in is filled with monsters," Dwayne said. "Bilal was the person who made me realize that what you think might be true about being in prison is not true."

There's a term for what Dwayne experienced: *moral elevation*. According to the psychologist Jonathan Haidt, moral elevation is the warm sensation we feel when witnessing another person's moral beauty—their kindness, courage, or self-sacrifice, for example. It's what we might experience when we see a first responder run into a burning building, or when we observe a child on the playground defend their friend from bullying. It's the admiration we feel when we see a person's perseverance in the face of a terminal illness or their caregiver's devotion. It's the moment when someone's extraordinary actions challenge our understanding of the world and force us to adjust our mental models to accommodate this new information, cracking open our imagination about what is possible.

If you're mourning the loss of certain possible selves or are fearing the selves you might become, it can be helpful to seek out other people's moral beauty. You can find inspiration by engaging with their stories, or by reflecting on the remarkable acts you've encountered in the past. In thinking about Dwayne's interaction with Bilal, I realized that I'd experienced an instance of moral elevation in 2015, after the horrific, racially motivated shooting at Mother Emanuel AME Church in Charleston, South Carolina. In a courtroom shortly after the tragedy, Nadine Collier, whose mother had been killed in the shooting, publicly extended her forgiveness to the killer. "You took something very precious away from me," Collier said. "I will never be able to talk to her again. I will never be able to hold her again. But I forgive you. And have mercy on your soul." I was stunned by her words. In that moment, she tapped into a greater depth of forgiveness than I'd thought possible.

Moral elevation is hard to experience on demand. You can't engineer that precise moment when someone else's strength of character will alter your perspective in just the ways you need. Fortunately, there are other methods you can use to conjure up new possible selves. Reading fiction is one, as it offers a kind of "identity laboratory" where you're given the opportunity to experiment with different versions of yourself. According to researchers like Jan Alber and María-Ángeles Martínez, readers blend their self-identities with the identities of a book's characters, and this dynamic interplay allows readers to freely try on new personality traits or to explore how they might respond to particular events or environments. Through fiction, write the researcher Cristina Loi and her colleagues, we are able to "temporarily expand the boundaries of our self by suspending the limitations of our personal identity."

You can also deliberately introduce yourself to ideas and perspectives from unfamiliar fields. During the summer before college, when I finally had to accept that my hand injury had extinguished all Violinist Maya selves, my dad gave me some good advice. "Maya, you've been effectively wearing blinders for the past ten years," he said. "Your job is to expose yourself to as many ideas as you can, with the most open mind possible." He encouraged me to read books, talk to people, and watch documentaries—and to do it all without a specific end goal in mind. I took his advice, and it was during this exploratory phase that I encountered the first book I ever read about the science of the mind, Steven Pinker's *The Language Instinct*. Reading this book is what eventually gave rise to a new possible self: Cognitive Scientist Maya.

Another way to imagine new possible selves is to think about how the skills and knowledge you've cultivated so far might be relevant in other domains. When I lost the violin, none of the technical skills I'd acquired could transfer over to potential future Mayas, but the general abilities I'd developed along the way—things like grit, creativity, and performing under pressure—were useful in many other pursuits, including in my role as a scientist. A good question you can ask yourself during a period of transition is: Who else can this person be?

A few weeks after Dwayne's encounter with *The Black Poets*, he learned that Knight had been found guilty of robbery in 1960 and had served an eight-year sentence at the Indiana State Prison. "Oh, so he *was* actually in prison," Dwayne recalled realizing. "I think a lot about what the other authors in *The Black Poets* wrote and how it moved me, but they didn't make me think I could *be* them. With Knight, I thought, *Oh, damn—I could really do this.*"

Dwayne found a manila folder and began adding poems and ideas to it as he came across them. Soon, his own writing filled the folder. Trying to put his experience into words gave him purpose, even as his circumstances grew worse. A super-maximum-security prison had recently opened, and inmates from nearby prisons, including Dwayne, were transferred there. Although the prison was new, it had already developed a reputation for having exceptionally cruel and racist guards. There were rumors that these guards had beaten and dragged prisoners across the prison yard naked and had even killed some of them. When Dwayne arrived, his cellmate explained how to get transferred to a mental institution as a means of escaping the violence. "You just need to rub feces on your face," he instructed Dwayne.

The only thing that kept Dwayne from despair was his commitment to writing. He read dozens of books and treated them as sacred objects, never opening them fully lest he crack their spines. He wrote poems as though they were his daily exercise. When he'd written enough pages, he'd stack and bind them together to create a book using thread from a torn-up sheet. "I went to books and my own writing to find the voices that would speak to me," he said. "And sometimes that work drove me to frustration, left me unsettled by the discovery of all I hadn't known before. I was moved both by the words of others and by those rare times when I'd turn a phrase myself that made me smile." In his first year at the supermax prison, he wrote more than a thousand poems.

Five years into his sentence, at the age of twenty-one, Dwayne was transferred to a lower-security prison in Augusta, Georgia. He signed up for a writing class there, which gave him an idea: he would send his poems to poets he admired, on the off chance that they would reply and provide feedback. He hadn't expected any responses, but one day he received a letter from the North Carolina poet Tony Hoagland. Hoagland had published an article in *The American Poetry Review* about what it meant to write with anger, and it had resonated with Dwayne. In his letter, Hoagland wrote that he believed Dwayne had promise as a poet. He also shared how poetry had saved his own life. Dwayne knew this to be true for him, too. "When I'd gotten my first book of poems, *The Black Poets* by Dudley Randall, I was a seventeen-year-old kid in a solitary confinement cell wondering if he was going to survive prison," Dwayne would later write. "By the time Mr. Hoagland wrote me, I was a few years away from release and still standing."

Dwayne began submitting his work to poetry magazines. In the letters that accompanied each submission, he wrote that even if the editors didn't accept his poems, he would nevertheless appreciate their advice on how he could improve. He also started sharing his poetry with other inmates, often reading his drafts aloud to them in the common area. Sometimes he even got them to write poetry with him. Soon, the other inmates gave Dwayne the nickname Professor.

Dwayne received one rejection letter after another. But one day, a piece of mail slid under his cell door from a literary magazine called *Poet Lore.* The editors wanted to publish Dwayne's poem "A Different Route," about a father who, after serving a lengthy prison sentence, takes his two children back to their old neighborhood with the hope of reclaiming what they had lost there.

Dwayne was beside himself. He ran into the common area and jumped up onto one of the chairs, waving the letter in his hand. "I'm published, man!" he exclaimed. "I'm a writer!" As his fellow inmates cheered, he was overcome with emotion. He had given voice not just to his life but to all their lives: "I was celebrating as though I represented everybody."

.

In the aftermath of a change, it can be challenging to feel our way into a new identity. The process is not unlike how many of us operate in our adolescence—years spent exploring, experimenting, soaking up knowledge and experiences, and gradually incorporating those pieces into a coherent self.

When Christine Hà was twenty-four years old, she was diagnosed with a rare autoimmune condition that caused her to go blind. As she lost her vision, Christine grew despondent: so many of the futures she'd previously imagined for herself disappeared, including the ones in which she was a passionate cook. She had been raised in a

Vietnamese American family, and as a child she loved the traditional, complex dishes her mom had cooked for her. When Christine moved into her first apartment at the age of nineteen, she began learning how to re-create those dishes. The more she cooked, the more it fulfilled her. She loved the process of discovery, the satisfaction of building new skills, and, of course, the final product, which she'd regularly share with friends and family at joyful gatherings. Making these dishes also carried symbolic value for her—it was a way to reconnect with her mom, whom she'd lost to cancer when she was a teenager. Being an ambitious cook had been a part of nearly every future Christine had imagined for herself. But now, with her vision rapidly deteriorating, she reluctantly concluded that those possible selves were gone.

Since Christine lived alone, though, she had no choice but to at least learn how to make some basic meals without her sight. She figured that the easiest thing to try was a peanut-butter-and-jelly sandwich. But she made a complete mess, with jelly ending up all over her hands and on the counter. "I remember being very frustrated with myself, throwing that sandwich away and just telling myself, 'I don't think I'll be able to ever cook again,'" she said.

Then Christine made a choice. She let herself feel upset, but did so with the resolve that as soon as she was in a better headspace, she would try to make something again. She set small, concrete goals, like learning how to cut an orange or scramble eggs. At first, she ended up with uneven orange slices or burned eggs, but she made it a point to appreciate that she'd achieved even that. Over time, she noticed that she was making considerable progress using this approach.

As the years passed, Christine developed confidence in the kitchen and started blogging about her experience under the name the Blind Cook. Her ambition grew as she tried out new recipes and techniques. By engaging her other senses and focusing on things like the sizzling sounds in the pan, how the food felt against the end of her cooking utensil, and how the spices smelled, she was able to create dishes that tasted far better than any she'd made before. "I actually think with my sense of sight out of the picture, I became much more of a nuanced cook in the kitchen," she said. Her blog caught the attention of the casting directors of *MasterChef*, and Christine went on to win season 3 of the show. These days, she owns two restaurants and has published a cookbook. When I asked if she would have her vision permanently restored if it were possible, she said no. She shared that while she'd like it back for about a week—so she could see her husband, dog, and friends, as well as what Justin Bieber and Ariana Grande look like—it's hard for her to imagine her life any other way now. She also loves the thrill of mastering new challenges without sight: snowboarding and rock climbing are her current favorites.

Christine was eventually able to work her way toward a possible self that had once felt unattainable. Indeed, as you navigate a change, it can seem as if there's a chasm between you and your aspirational self. In these cases, it can be helpful to break down a larger ambition into smaller, highly specific goals, as Christine and Dwayne did when they broke "becoming a chef" and "becoming a poet" into goals like learning how to cut an orange or writing poetry every day. Smaller goals give you a sense of accomplishment in the shorter term and prove that you are in fact capable of embodying a new identity.

They're also less subject to what the behavioral science professor Ayelet Fishbach calls the *middle problem*: people are typically highly motivated at the beginning of pursuing a goal, when they're still excited and haven't yet encountered any significant challenges, as well as near the end, when they can see the finish line, but they tend to experience a lull in motivation in the middle. Setting shorter-term goals reduces the length of each "middle" stretch, which allows you to spend less continuous time in a lower-motivation state and to return to a higher-motivation state sooner. For example, by creating a weekly goal as opposed to a yearly one, you spend just over two straight days in a lower-motivation state rather than four straight months.

After setting your goal, if you're struggling to make progress toward your new possible self, you can tap into the power of two evidence-based techniques introduced by the behavioral science professor Katy Milkman and her colleagues. The first is to capitalize on what is known as the *fresh start effect* by initiating your goal pursuit at a time that naturally feels like a new beginning. This can be calendar-based, like the first day of the week or your birthday, or at a transition point in your life, like moving to a different city or accepting a new job. During fresh starts, people are more capable of breaking from past patterns of behavior and establishing new ones. The second technique is known as *temptation bundling*. This is when you pair a challenging task, which may deliver gratification only in the longer term (for example, working out), with an existing behavior that you find immediately rewarding (for example, listening to your favorite music). If you're finding it hard to go running, for instance, you might allow yourself to listen to your favorite music while on these runs—

but critically *only* on these runs, so that the reward becomes exclusively paired with the challenging task. Research shows that temptation bundling successfully incentivizes people to keep returning to the challenge.

Another tactic for following through on your goals involves taking advantage of a quirk in the way the brain forms memories. Interestingly, when you reflect back on how pleasurable an experience was, not all moments are created equal. You give greater weight to the emotional *peak* of the experience—the moment that was the most intense, either positive or negative—and to the *end* of the experience. This is called the *peak-end rule,* and it was formulated by Daniel Kahneman, a Nobel Prize–winning psychologist, and his colleagues. The upshot here is that you can alter how you look back on an event by more deliberately shaping its emotional peak and its end. You might tack on something joyful to the end of, say, a tough work session or otherwise make the ending slightly less difficult or painful. By strategically structuring your memories in this way, you can look back more favorably on the session, making it more likely that you'll return to pursuing your goal.

And finally, you can help realize your new possible self by forging a community with the right people. When you're part of a group that believes in your new identity, their shared vision can lift you when you're unsure of yourself, or reinforce your identity when you do succeed, as when Dwayne's fellow inmates celebrated his becoming a published author. About a month after the writer Nora McInerny's husband died, she was introduced to a woman who'd also lost her husband and had a similar aversion to the "widow" label. Soon, the two of them decided to create a support group called the Hot Young Widows Club, an irreverent challenge to the negative stereotypes associated with people who've lost their partners. The people in Nora's community were able to try on various identities without judgment and to even coauthor new possible selves together.

·

Dwayne was released from prison in 2005 at the age of twenty-four, roughly a year after he published his first poem. Since he'd earned his high school diploma while incarcerated, he was able to enroll in Prince George's Community College in Maryland. He also got a job at Karibu Books, an independent bookstore, where he started the YoungMenRead book club for Black kids in the community. He then went on to earn a BA from the University of Maryland, an MFA in creative writing from Warren Wilson College in North Carolina, and a law degree from Yale. In 2009, he published *A Question of Freedom: A Memoir of Learning, Survival, and Coming of Age in Prison*, which he followed with several poetry collections, including *Bastards of the Reagan Era* and *Felon*. In 2012, President Barack Obama appointed him to a task force on restoring juvenile justice and preventing delinquency. Dwayne was told he was the first-ever formerly incarcerated person to receive such an appointment.

But his criminal record has followed him throughout these experiences. Dwayne applied to Howard University after his second year in community college and was accepted on a full scholarship, but he said that it fell through once he revealed that he'd been incarcerated.

After he graduated from Yale Law School and passed the bar exam, the Connecticut Bar Association sent him a letter saying that he would need to prove his "character and fitness" to practice as an attorney, due to his time in prison. Dwayne cried when he received the letter. (He pulled together recommendations from professors and former prisoners and was eventually sworn in as an attorney at a courthouse in New Haven.) At times, he has struggled to get job offers or approval to rent apartments. When he went on a second date with his future wife, he worried that disclosing his past might end their budding romance. His prison sentence was not just something he carried in the world—it was something everyone he loved would need to carry too.

And yet Dwayne has found more richness both inside and outside his identity as a former prisoner than he could have imagined. He remains committed to supporting his friends who are still incarcerated, and as their lawyer, he's helped many of them secure early parole. My conversations with him were frequently interrupted by calls from prison, which he always accepted. In 2020, he created a nonprofit called Freedom Reads, which builds small libraries in prisons, juvenile facilities, and immigrant detention centers across the United States. The libraries' books, which range from Gabriel García Márquez's *One Hundred Years of Solitude* to Andre Agassi's memoir, are placed on shelves carved from walnut, maple, and cherry wood, an intentional design choice meant to counteract the bleakness of prison. There are now more than four hundred libraries in nearly fifty institutions. One superintendent who'd worked in the system for decades told Dwayne that he was eager to participate in the library project because he had never come across anything beautiful inside of a prison. In 2021, Dwayne was awarded a MacArthur Fellowship, informally known as the "Genius Grant."

Dwayne still thinks about Bilal's influence nearly thirty years later. Writing has been a way for Dwayne to process both the atrocities and the humanity he observed while in prison. He feels compelled to share his stories as a means of honoring the people he's met along the way, especially those who still remain behind bars. "Poetry," he said, "is a medium of caring."

In his poems, Dwayne often uses an interesting device: he writes in the first person, even when he's writing about something he himself has never experienced. "I barely see my daughters at all these days. / Out here caught up, lost in an old cliché," he writes in one poem, though Dwayne has been a devoted and present father to his two young sons. He does this because he believes that if he implicates himself in society's ills, then he—and his readers—will feel responsible for finding solutions. It's a way of advocating for people whose stories merit empathy and attention. "When you read a poem out loud in the first person, in all the uncomfortable imagining, the line blurs between you and them," he said. Dwayne is standing at the scratch line for others, as Knight once did for Gerald, and as Bilal once did for Jamil.

3

Mental Spirals

One foggy Sunday morning, Matt Gutman was making pancakes for his kids when he received a call from his boss at ABC News. It was January 2020, and Matt had just returned home to L.A. after a month of reporting on the road as the network's chief national correspondent. When he picked up the phone, his boss told him that the basketball player Kobe Bryant had been in a fatal helicopter crash about fifteen miles from Matt's home. ABC needed Matt to cover the developing story. He grabbed supplies while checking news alerts and texting the local sheriff, then jumped in his car and drove off.

As he got closer to the scene, he was overcome by the responsibility of delivering this tragic news to millions of viewers. His heart began to pound against his rib cage, faster and faster. His hands trembled. His chest tightened. His vision narrowed. Sweat seeped through his clothes. He tried to breathe, but he felt as though he could not remember how. He was having a panic attack.

The sensation wasn't new. In his twenty years as a journalist, Matt had experienced panic attacks more than a hundred times. To rein in his panic before he went live on air, he'd developed coping mechanisms like meditating, doing push-ups, smoking a cigarette, and sometimes even wearing his "lucky" underwear. Somehow, he'd always found a way to work through it once the cameras started rolling. He'd recover his composure enough to deliver the full story live on TV, even if it came out in stammers or between labored breaths, and was usually reassured to find that viewers hadn't noticed anything was off.

Matt's panic attacks never happened when he was in physical danger. They were rooted in a different kind of threat: the risk of social judgment. He had reported without issue from war zones, from cartel-controlled territories, and within the wreckage of hurricanes and tornadoes. He knew that in these extenuating circumstances, his colleagues and viewers did not expect a perfect performance and would forgive any fumbles. Instead, his panic emerged in situations in which he knew that people had higher expectations of him.

On the morning of the helicopter crash, Matt could feel the pressure of the public's expectations mounting within him—he had to get the story just right. As he prepared to go live, he counseled himself: *Deep breath in. Deep breath out.* But as the broadcast started, his panic only intensified. Matt's colleague opened the segment by telling viewers that he'd received confirmation that the NBA legend Kobe Bryant had died in a helicopter crash in Southern California.

He then passed it over to Matt to share any other known details about the crash, which had taken the lives of all those on board. "We know that it happened about an hour ago . . ." Matt began. His mind was scrambled and on hyperdrive, his heart still racing. His words came tumbling out. "The fact that four of his children are believed to be on that helicopter with him, all daughters, one of them a newborn," he continued, "is simply devastating."

But the claim that Bryant's four daughters were with him was incorrect; nine people had been on board and only one of them was Bryant's child—his thirteen-year-old, Gianna. Matt did not even realize he'd made the error—the whole broadcast was one big blur in his mind—until a colleague frantically texted him after the segment cut away.

As soon as he could, Matt jumped back on the air to issue a correction and apologize for any pain his mistake might have caused. But the damage was done. In what was already a devastating tragedy, Matt's error had only compounded the public's confusion and distress. Two days later, network executives called him and imposed a one-month suspension for his misreporting.

Matt readily accepted the punishment. In the weeks that followed, he was filled with self-recrimination. He spent his empty days at home, alone with his thoughts. As he saw it, his suspension had been inevitable, even long overdue. For years, he'd been walking a tightrope, and now, at last, he'd fallen off. With his wife at work and his kids at school, he paced around the house, walked the dogs, and occasionally worked out. But he also set up a Google alert that notified him every time a new article about his mistake came out. He scoured the web and read the comments from angry viewers. The public was skewering him, questioning not just his competence but also his morality. Some commenters said that ABC should fire him. Others said that he should be permanently banished from journalism.

At night, unable to sleep, Matt spiraled. What was wrong with him? He had delivered plenty of imperfect broadcasts over the years as a result of his panic, and although he'd felt a "shame hangover" each time, he'd always found a way through it. This time was different, though: he had made a serious journalistic error. He'd thought his panic was something he could manage, but now it was clear that he'd been wrong.

A new thought took hold of Matt: maybe his brain was fundamentally broken. Maybe his panic meant that *he* was broken. The idea seized him completely, holding his mind hostage hour after hour, day after day. The public criticism only legitimized and strengthened his conviction. "It was this perverse vindication," he recalls thinking, "that I was irredeemable."

•

Most of us know what it's like to get caught in a negative mental spiral. Any number of things can trigger these unrelenting, suffocating loops, but the catalyst is typically a change in our lives. Our new anxieties, regrets, and uncertainties can take on a life of their own and become a bigger challenge to deal with than the change itself. These thoughts become like mind worms, nestling into our psyches, hijacking our attention, and stoking our biggest fears. *What's wrong with me? How could I not have seen that coming? How could they do that to me? What's going to happen?*

This is known as *rumination*, and it can involve obsessively rehashing something in the past, grappling with perceived problems in the present, or catastrophizing an imagined future. When we're in its grip, it can be hard to focus on anything else or to conceive of ever moving past our problem. Rumination is a common symptom of conditions like depression and anxiety, but anyone can fall into its trap from time to time.

Part of the allure of fixating on a particular problem is that analysis and self-reflection often *do* bear fruit. But when we ruminate, we're not actually making progress toward a solution: we're simply cycling through the same negative thoughts over and over again. Each time we engage with our problem, though, we can fall prey to the illusion that we're on the verge of a breakthrough—that we're just about to gain some great insight, find closure, or attain some guarantee of security. *If I analyze my mistake enough, I'll avoid repeating the mistake in the future. If I dwell on this failure, I'll feel like I have paid my penance and can move on. If I catalog all the harms that may affect my family, I'll be able to keep them safe.*

Similar to when we're in denial or think that our possible selves have been predetermined, rumination puts blinders on us. We are trapped within a narrow understanding of our situation and are unable to see that there are other ways to approach it. As Matt did when he scoured the web for negative comments about himself, we might search only for further evidence that confirms our worries. This can lead us to double down on our convictions, however unfounded they might be.

So, what does it take to break free from these maddening mental spirals? If you've ever experienced rumination, you likely know that the brute-force approach of telling yourself to "just stop already" usually makes things worse. What does work, it turns out, is a technique called *psychological distancing*. As researched by psychologists like Ethan Kross and Ozlem Ayduk, psychological distancing involves creating space between yourself and the thoughts that have taken hold. In other words, since rumination arises from zooming *in* too closely on a situation, one of the best ways to break free from it is to actively zoom *out*. This distance allows you to see your situation from new angles, which can release you from rumination's hamster wheel.

Zooming out involves proactively seeking other points of view or greater context so that you can approach your problems more constructively. Just as there are different ways you can fall into ruminative loops, there are also many ways you can spring out from them.

•

When Matt's suspension was over, he returned to work. But as he tried to steel himself through each broadcast, he couldn't shed his belief that he was broken. A new question also bubbled up in his mind: Why did broken people like him even exist? "This panic thing had derailed me," Matt said. "And so I suddenly became consumed with trying to understand why it has persisted in our genetic code, and why we haven't evolved out of it."

In the year following his mistake, Matt decided to interview as many experts as he could who might have an answer to his question. One afternoon, while on a reporting trip, he returned to his hotel room and hopped on a Zoom call with Randolph Nesse, a professor at Arizona State University who is a leader in the field of evolutionary psychiatry. Matt confessed to Nesse his belief that he was a faulty human and that his panic attacks were the product of a glitch in the genetic code. Nesse listened attentively, and then offered a counterargument. The ability to panic, he told Matt, was not a glitch but an asset. In fact, it was one of the reasons humans have been able to survive for so long.

Nesse explained that the stress hormones we release in response to panic, which lead to things like a racing heart and increased respiration, are essential for reacting appropriately to danger. These physiological changes send more oxygen into the bloodstream, enabling us to move more quickly out of harm's way. Rapid spikes in cortisol and adrenaline, meanwhile, increase our alertness. As Nesse spoke, Matt nodded along. He could understand that logic, but he was panicking even when it didn't make sense to. Surely this still made him broken, right?

Again, Nesse had a reassuring reply. Because there can be uncertainty about whether a situation is actually dangerous—*What was that rustle from behind that bush?*—it can be better, in the long run, to overreact than to underreact. From an evolutionary perspective, Nesse said, it is more adaptive for our brains to respond to a thousand false alarms than to miss a single real one. In times past, someone who was more inclined to overreact than the average person might have saved their tribe from danger.

But Matt did not panic in response to potential physical threats; he panicked over his fears of social judgment. How could Nesse justify that? Here, too, Nesse had an answer. Our ancestors didn't survive just by worrying about threats from wild animals or natural disasters; they also needed to worry about being cast out of their group. For most of history, humans were able to survive only by banding together, and so our brains became primed to detect social threats as well. This explained why Matt was hyper-attuned to other people's perceptions of him, and why he panicked when he felt as though his social standing might be in jeopardy.

Matt had sought out Nesse to understand why he was broken, but Nesse helped Matt zoom out by encouraging him to question this assumption altogether and to contextualize his panic within the larger story of human evolution. When we're stuck in rumination, a powerful first step is to stop and interrogate our assumptions. It's easy to forget that our ways of thinking are limited by the boundaries of our personal experience, knowledge, and beliefs. By sharing our concerns with other people and encouraging them to poke holes in our narratives, we can encounter new perspectives that help us forge new mental pathways. Might there be a different conclusion to draw? A different story from the one we've been telling ourselves?

As Matt left the call with Nesse, his body relaxed. His tendency to panic didn't mean he was broken after all. It meant he *wasn't* broken. It was clear, though, that his system needed a serious recalibration. Being *this* prone to panic had negatively affected his mental well-being and had threatened his livelihood. But he could at least let go of his self-loathing. "I could stop hating my mind," he said.

Matt's process of reworking his relationship with his panic is an example of *cognitive reappraisal*, in which deliberately changing how we interpret a situation can alter its emotional impact. As a result of his reappraisal, Matt was able to take a more constructive approach toward managing his panic attacks. This included cognitive-behavioral therapy and selective serotonin reuptake inhibitors (SSRIs), which are first-line treatments when a person's rumination is serious enough to compromise their mental health, as well as breathwork and guided psychedelic trips. Over time, Matt's panic episodes have become less frequent and intense, and his "I'm broken" script no longer has such a hold over him. "For decades, I had a drill sergeant in my head who was always hollering at me and insulting me," he said. "I still have an inner drill sergeant, but this one never screams at me, and he never tells me I'm unworthy."

Today, Matt is thriving in his role as ABC's chief national correspondent and reports live from around the globe. He now sees an upside to his anxiety. The fact that he is hyperaware of what other people may be thinking has enabled him to be a more compassionate, perceptive listener. "I'm often meeting people on the worst day of their lives, and I'm able to speak to them in a common language," he said. "It's one of the reasons they can trust me with their stories."

•

Matt's rumination focused on himself and his perceived brokenness, but change can also trigger rumination about the world outside ourselves. This is what happened to my friend Kylie Yorke, who has been passionate about the outdoors since childhood. The summer after her junior year of college, Kylie worked as a guide at a nature-based therapy organization for kids near Lake Tahoe. "I loved the natural rhythms of day and nightfall, fresh air, self-reliance, resourcefulness, and this deeply rooted feeling that this is how we were meant to live," she said.

One afternoon, as she hiked up a mountain with a group of kids, they could smell smoke. On the horizon, they saw a wildfire blazing. Kylie, who had grown up outside Los Angeles, was acquainted with wildfires; ash had rained down on her high school for two days after a blaze in Northern California. But she had never seen the devastation of a fire up close. A few days later, she went for a run along the river and was saddened by what she encountered. "The forest I'd grown familiar with was reduced to charcoal stubs," she said. "The scene around me was apocalyptic, starved of life."

Kylie knew that wildfires were a natural part of the forest life cycle, but she also knew that climate change was increasing their frequency and severity. There was something about coming face-to-face with this specific fire's destruction and witnessing an entire community forced to flee their homes that transformed Kylie's intellectual concern about the future of the planet into a visceral one.

When Kylie expressed this concern to her coworkers, they shrugged.

Many of them had experienced devastating fire seasons before and had become desensitized. But Kylie's fixation only increased, and she soon grew despondent. She'd always loved going on walks and soaking in the sounds around her. Now, though, the birds chirping or the breeze rustling through leaves left her sad and anxious, as she imagined they might one day no longer exist. She berated herself for taking flights and driving a car, activities that contributed to carbon emissions. On visits home to see her parents and her brother, she sat in silence at the dinner table, her eyes glazed over. "My mind was so far in doom land that I found it hard to focus on most other conversations," she said.

When she returned to college that fall, she reached out to her thesis adviser. Kylie was a double major in psychology and philosophy and had been planning to write a thesis about the environment. But now she had more questions than answers. "How do we stay happy while simultaneously engaging with our eco-anxiety?" she asked in an email. "How can we convince people to engage with such a distressing matter in the first place?"

As part of her thesis research, Kylie read *Sapiens*, by Yuval Noah Harari. A sweeping survey of humankind, the book explores human nature and the causes of some of the most important developments and revolutions in history. Reading it, Kylie had a realization: "Human beings have been facing existential threats for as long as we've existed as a species," Kylie said, "and we've often risen to meet those challenges by engaging in collective action." She was especially heartened to read a newspaper article about the sixteen million Americans who enlisted in the military, as well as those who signed up for factory work, during World War II. And it wasn't just that people could rally together when they already believed in a cause; history also showed that large numbers of people could change their minds about whether to care about a cause in the first place.

Kylie's dread began to give way to hope. If humans had radically improved society before, they could do it again, and she could be part of that effort. "We study history not to know the future," Harari writes, "but to widen our horizons, to understand that our present situation is neither natural nor inevitable, and that we consequently have many more possibilities before us than we imagine."

Looking to history is one way of engaging in *mental time travel*, which research shows is an effective way of creating psychological distance. You can mentally travel back in time, as Kylie did, and contextualize present-day challenges within the larger story of human history. You can also travel into the past of your own life story, revisiting moments in which you displayed resilience or overcame adversity, to encourage you in the present. Alternatively, you can mentally travel to the future by imagining how you will feel about your current problem in, say, a month, a year, or decades from now. Traveling into the future is particularly helpful when you're dealing with challenges in your personal life that may feel less significant to you over time, or even go away. (By contrast, it would of course not be helpful in the context of climate change.) If you're ruminating over a tense exchange with a difficult coworker, for instance, it can be beneficial to reflect on whether you'll care as much about the exchange five years from now as you do today. This can remind you that your current situation is transient. When my own rumination has been at its worst, however, I've found myself believing that I would still be obsessed with a problem well into the future. In these cases, it's been useful to reflect on times in the past when I was similarly convinced that I would never break out of the cycle of rumination, but I turned out to be wrong. Reminding myself of this fact has helped me gain distance from my current preoccupations.

For Kylie, using mental time travel has freed up energy that she has since been able to direct toward addressing the problem of climate change. For her thesis, she wrote about the psychological and social reasons why people don't take more climate action. She now does research in social psychology about the role that hope can play in motivating pro-environmental behaviors. She is optimistic that her findings will bring comfort to those who, like her, have felt despair about the future of the planet. "I can't stop every forest from burning, but I can contribute to a future where fewer do," she said. "I still feel grief, but I'm now more curious about how and why we got here and what a future could look like."

Florence Williams was preparing dinner with her husband one evening when she asked about her father-in-law, who had recently fallen ill. Her husband took out his phone to show Florence an email with a health update, but he accidentally pulled up an email in which he'd proclaimed his love to another woman.

Florence was shaken to her core. She and her husband had built a happy life in the thirty-two years they'd been a couple. They had raised two thoughtful and loving children and had so many rich memories together. Sure, they'd had their share of ups and downs, but that was true of most marriages. Florence had always felt, deep down, that they would spend the rest of their lives together.

In her anger and grief, she interrogated her husband about what had happened. He admitted that he had indeed fallen for another woman and that they'd had an emotional affair. But he said that he still loved Florence, and that he valued the life they'd created. Florence was desperate to save her marriage and was determined to forgive him. She persuaded him to do couples therapy with her, but after months of counseling he decided that he wanted to be with his "real soulmate," and that Florence wasn't that person. He asked for a divorce.

Florence was devastated. How had the life she'd worked so hard for turned to cinders? What signs had she missed? How could her husband destroy everything they shared? She fell into an extreme state of anxiety. She lost weight, had trouble sleeping, and developed an autoimmune condition.

Florence had a background as a science journalist, and so her instinct was to find a way to "fix" her heartbreak: she decided she would analyze what exactly had gone wrong, and when, and why. Only by attaining this kind of clarity would she be able to heal. With this goal in mind, she set out on a fourteen-day solo canoe trip, hoping that the solitude would offer her some insight and peace of mind. But as she sat alone on a rocky ledge overlooking the river, replaying scenes from her marriage and scribbling down reflections in a notebook, she grew only more agitated. In her effort to gain closure, she gravitated toward overly simple, extreme narratives. In a short period, she went from believing that the collapse of her marriage was entirely her husband's fault to thinking it was entirely *her* fault. She spiraled into a vortex of self-blame: *I was too neurotic. I was impatient with his needs. I didn't communicate what I wanted. I wasn't fun enough.* By the end of the trip, Florence was exasperated.

When the relationships in our lives change unexpectedly, it's easy to start ruminating. *Did they mean to say that? Why did I respond like that? Were they always this way? What could I have done differently?* We crave definitive answers, mining our memories and revisiting old conversations in our heads to try to resolve any ambiguity. If we could just figure out why they stopped talking to us, or loving us, we could move on. If we could just figure out how to prevent another betrayal, we might be able to let this one go. If we could just figure out a way to hate them or blame them for the demise of the relationship, we might feel better. We want to solve a problem by doing more analysis when more analysis isn't the solution.

Loneliness can set off or intensify rumination, as it did for Florence. This is especially true in times of significant change, when we're untethered from our familiar relationships, environments, and routines. Without the usual landmarks to orient ourselves, it's common to look inward and fixate on our negative thoughts. The reverse is also true: rumination can exacerbate loneliness. As we struggle to untangle whatever complicated knot our mind has tied, we may begin to believe we're exceptional—that we're the only ones grappling with this specific problem in this specific way. But we can take steps to shift this perception: connecting more deeply with other people can not only tame the feeling that we're alone in our struggles but also open us up to the lessons these same people might teach us.

About a year after her divorce, Florence serendipitously stumbled upon such an opportunity. While she was in Slovenia for a conference, she noticed that there was a museum just a train ride away in Croatia called the Museum of Broken Relationships. It chronicles stories of failed love and displays artifacts donated by the brokenhearted that pay homage to old relationships—from an unworn wedding dress to a toaster stolen from an ex during a breakup. Florence decided to visit the museum.

In one exhibit, she came across the story of a woman who'd been with her husband since she was a teenager. Thirty years into their marriage, he confessed that he had never loved her at all and had fallen in love with someone else. The woman, whose exhibit featured a stuffed animal her husband had gifted her when she was seventeen, described her utter bewilderment at what had happened. As Florence continued through the museum, she saw just how many of these lovelorn tales were filled with unresolved questions and unmended hearts. "That shock of recognition that something that can feel so singular is actually universal was comforting," she said.

It was here that Florence finally zoomed out. She was able to step outside her own story and see how so much of what she had experienced—the obsession with needing answers, the melodrama, the self-loathing, the anger, the fixation on past mistakes—was present in the narratives of others. "I started to see, 'Oh, everyone tells themselves stories of woe,'" she said. "All of our minds go to these dark, crazy places for a little while. And when it's not your story, you can also see a little bit of humor in it all."

Florence discovered, too, that connecting with other broken-hearted people opened her up to a fundamental lesson contained within the museum's stories: finding resolution around her heartbreak—achieving what psychologists call *cognitive closure*—was an impossible goal that she should try to let go of. Her shift in mindset has since had positive spillover effects in other areas of her life—a life she no longer sees as one big puzzle to solve. "I've learned that life is full of unknowable answers, and that there's sometimes something beautiful in the mystery of it all," she said.

•

When Ramsey Khabbaz was a twenty-year-old college student, he woke up one morning to a high-pitched, continuous ringing. The tone was piercing. It took Ramsey a few seconds to realize that the sound was coming from inside his head. Curiously, he could hear the ringing only in his left ear. Had he fallen asleep with an earbud in? He poked his finger in his ear. Nothing. Ramsey jumped up and down on his left leg with his head tilted to the side, hoping to dislodge whatever was trapped in there. But nothing fell out, and the ringing persisted.

Ramsey was unnerved, yet he didn't have time to dwell on the situation. He was already late to his video-production internship, which he'd started the week before. He was a film and English double major and an aspiring movie director; this internship was an important first step in his career. Doing his best to ignore his physical discomfort,

Ramsey found his way to the office, hopeful that he would be back to normal soon. But as the day went on he noticed that he had also lost all hearing in his left ear. It was impossible to drown out the ringing with music or white noise. Ramsey's mom drove him to his primary-care doctor, who referred Ramsey to see an ear specialist the following day.

The next morning, Ramsey again awoke to the same maddening ringing. He lay there for a moment, reflecting on what it'd been like to wake up to a state of calm every morning for the past two decades—how he'd luxuriate in bed for a bit, listening to the birds chirping outside or trying to recapture the last few seconds of a dream. Now he was waking up to a blaring alarm that never shut off. It was the sound of imminent threat, of emergency.

The ear specialist diagnosed Ramsey with tinnitus and "sudden sensorineural hearing loss" in his left ear, and prescribed steroids to restore some of the hearing loss. The doctor could not explain the cause but rattled off some possibilities: Maybe it was an unusual autoimmune response to a virus or the residual effect of a concussion? Or maybe it was a brain tumor? This would be unusual at Ramsey's age, but the specialist scheduled an MRI. As Ramsey slid into the dark tunnel of the machine, he felt like he was lying in a coffin.

He got a call later that afternoon from his doctor, who had reassuring news: Ramsey did not have a brain tumor. The doctor was still unsure as to the cause of Ramsey's symptoms and warned him that the ringing might be permanent. Ramsey knew that he should feel comforted—he didn't have a brain tumor! But the problem in his ear remained unexplained, and that troubled him. It had just . . . happened. His body had turned on him, and for no apparent reason.

What other terrible thing might strike him out of the blue? Would he actually get that brain tumor someday? And, if so, when? Tomorrow? The next day? A year from now?

When we ruminate, we build a mental prison for ourselves. Each repetitive thought lays down another brick, constructing walls that block out the world. After Matt's on-air mistake, he locked himself within a narrative of self-loathing. Kylie grew disconsolate as she conjured up apocalyptic visions of the planet and was unable to appreciate the rest of the human experience. Florence desperately searched for answers to the puzzle of her heartbreak, trapping herself in a futile quest for closure. And for Ramsey, his mental prison—born of his fear of unseen threats lurking in his body—was reinforced by the constant ringing. "The siren in my ear was a continual, gnawing reminder of what could happen," he said. "Of what *would* happen."

Ramsey met with half a dozen doctors for second and third and sixth opinions. If he could just pinpoint the cause of the ringing—a loud concert he'd forgotten about, or an ear infection the doctors had missed—then maybe he could regain some trust in his body. But the doctors had no answers. Ramsey holed up in his apartment, declining invitations to parties and other social gatherings. It was only when he learned that his neighborhood movie theater was hosting a "Big Screen Classics" series, about a month after the ringing began, that he mustered up the will to venture out. Ramsey loved this theater; it was where he'd grown up watching films with his family, and where he'd brought his girlfriend on some of their dates. Perhaps returning to this old haunt would bring him some comfort. He and his girlfriend bought tickets for a movie neither of them had seen,

Hannah and Her Sisters, a dramedy about three sisters and their romantic interests.

As they settled into their seats, Ramsey did his best to focus. The movie opens in a crowded Manhattan apartment where Hannah is hosting a large Thanksgiving dinner. A subplot soon emerges. Hannah's ex-husband, a TV writer named Mickey, experiences hearing loss and ringing in his ear one morning. A hypochondriac, he goes to a doctor, who orders a series of tests. While Mickey waits for the results, he also checks in with a doctor friend, who offhandedly mentions that his symptoms could be the result of a brain tumor. Mickey receives a clean bill of health soon afterward, but nevertheless falls into a spiral of existential dread.

Ramsey's jaw dropped. He elbowed his girlfriend—was she seeing what he was seeing? The movie played on. In one scene, Mickey, crippled by despair, wanders around the city and into a theater showing an old Groucho Marx film. As Mickey watches the movie, he loses himself in the comedy and begins to laugh, which deflates some of his despair. His joy makes him see that, even if his existential fears were justified, he'd still want to experience living. "You know, what the hell, it's not all a drag," he says. "And I'm thinking to myself, 'Jeez, I should stop ruining my life searching for answers I'm never gonna get, and just enjoy it while it lasts.'"

Ramsey was stunned. For him, going to the movie theater had always been the equivalent of going to church; it was a place where he could connect with people across time and space, and with new ways of seeing the world. And now it was as if the movies had crafted a custom-made message for him.

Ramsey worked to process Mickey's story. "What if the worst *is* true?" he asked himself. "What if my body continues to fail me without warning?" Like Mickey, Ramsey realized there would still be so much he would want to live for.

The feeling of wonder, reverence, and surrender that overcame Ramsey in the theater—in a word, the experience of *awe*—has a unique power to break the spell of rumination. Dacher Keltner, a leading expert on the science of awe, defines the emotion as "the feeling of being in the presence of something vast that transcends your current understanding of the world." This sense of vastness can be produced by anything that's larger than ourselves, physically or conceptually: the grandeur of an electric storm filling the sky, the elegance of a piece of music, the groundbreaking nature of a scientific discovery, the breathtaking design of a work of architecture, the consummate skill of an athlete. Encounters like these cause little earthquakes in our minds, prompting us to revise our existing assumptions about the world. For Ramsey, the coincidence of seeing a version of his life play out before him, through an art form he loved, at the exact moment he needed it, led him to reject his assumption that having a fallible body meant he could not enjoy his life.

Awe can quiet our mental chatter not just by challenging the beliefs that triggered our rumination in the first place but by diminishing our sense of self; neuroscience studies show that when we experience awe, activity in brain regions associated with self-focus decreases. This allows us to see beyond our individual wants, needs, and anxieties, and to internalize that we are part of a larger whole.

And so, when our negative thoughts get stuck in a loop, we can deliberately look for ways to experience awe. For some people, this may mean taking up a spiritual practice like prayer or meditation. For others, it may mean engaging with art or music, or experiencing the transcendence that can come with a guided psychedelic trip. Nature, too, is a perennial source of awe. The dance of a bumblebee, the snowcapped peaks of a mountain, and the expanse of the night sky can all subtly shift our attention outward. (You don't need access to majestic views to get the psychological benefits of nature, either. One study showed that patients recovering from surgery who were assigned to a room that looked out onto a set of trees healed faster and were evaluated as more emotionally resilient than patients whose rooms faced a brick wall.)

Today, Ramsey still hears the same high-pitched, continuous ringing in his left ear. The sound has not attenuated or changed in its quality, but as Ramsey has learned to quiet his existential fears, his relationship with the sound has changed. One morning at breakfast, about two years after the ringing first started, he noticed that he'd gone the entire previous day without thinking about it. "And that was inexplicable to me. It was so comforting to know that the tinnitus itself didn't need to go away in order for me to not be bothered by it," he said. "It's just my version of quiet now."

·

When a change occurs in our lives, our instinct may be to resist the uncertainty it brings and to try to resolve it. Often, this intolerance of uncertainty is what gives rise to mental spirals—our brains search in earnest for answers, despite the fact that there are none to be found. Rumination, in other words, can be an expression of a desire to assert control in situations where we simply have less of it than we'd like. The more we can strive to exist comfortably in life's gray spaces, the less likely it is that rumination will take hold.

The specific topic our rumination latches on to will vary throughout our lives. Each time we're stuck in a new loop, its novelty can give it a kind of power. Even if we've triumphed over previous bouts of rumination, it can feel like this new issue is somehow different and will resist all intervention. That's the devilish side of rumination: our brains will fool us into thinking that the topic we're currently perseverating over is the most threatening, most pressing issue we've faced, and that we have no defenses against this new foe.

This is why it can be useful to assemble a diverse anti-rumination tool kit. Different tools will work in different situations, and what worked last time may not work this time. In addition to the zooming-out techniques of cognitive reappraisal, mental time travel, and awe, another tool you can add to your kit is *affect labeling*. This involves taking a step back and trying to identify what negative emotions you're experiencing as a result of your rumination. Research shows that giving a negative feeling a specific label (for example, "frustration," "despair," or "envy") can reduce its intensity. Naming it fosters psychological distance by shifting your perception away from "being" the emotion to simply "having" the emotion.

Another tool for zooming out is *visual self-distancing*, in which you mentally view your situation from a "fly on the wall" perspective. For example, you might revisit that tense conversation with your coworker from earlier in the day, but this time you try to process it not from a first-person perspective but instead as an impartial observer. This approach has been shown to decrease emotional reactivity and to lower the frequency of intrusive thoughts. A related strategy is *distanced self-talk*, which you can practice in one of two ways. The first way, rooted in self-compassion research by the psychologist Kristin Neff, is to coach yourself through your situation as you might coach a friend: this can limit your self-berating and keep you focused on generating constructive advice. The second way is to refer to yourself in the third person—using your name—or in the second person, when guiding yourself through a problem. (For instance, "Maya, you need to get a grip!" rather than "I need to get a grip!") This tweak in framing has proved to be a powerful antidote to rumination in both high- and low-stress situations, for both past and future events, and across a wide range of negative emotions.

And finally, it's worth noting that engaging in activities that distract you from your negative emotions is not only okay but can be beneficial. One narrative that has become pervasive, particularly in Western conversations around wellness, is that the only healthy way to move on from a bad experience is to *approach* it—to fully confront, express, and process your negative emotions. Otherwise, you risk having those emotions resurface in the future with even greater force. But recent research on resilience reveals a more complex story in which individual differences play a big role in determining what makes for a healthy response in any given circumstance. The upshot of this research is that if directly and persistently confronting your negative emotions is working for you, stay the course. But if you're not gravitating toward that method and are doing fine—or if some combination of both approaching and avoiding your negative emotions is your sweet spot—there's no need to feel guilty or to fear that you will pay for it later. As the psychologist Ethan Kross writes, "If something doesn't keep cropping up, there's a good chance you're *not* harboring some invisible wound that will fester and ruin your life decades down the road."

When it comes to techniques to take your mind off things, as Michelle Obama writes in her book *The Light We Carry*, "sometimes you recognize a tool only after it starts working for you. And sometimes, it turns out, the smallest of tools can help us to sort through the largest of feelings." During the pandemic, she found that knitting helped lessen her rumination; for my sister, it was a combination of cooking and solving thousand-piece jigsaw puzzles. My old philosophy professor once told me that whenever he was overwhelmed by the weight of existential questions, he turned to test-prep books because there was some relief in being asked a question that had a right answer.

Recently, I ruminated over an issue I'd never struggled with before. At the outset of the COVID-19 pandemic, I developed insomnia. As I endured sleepless night after sleepless night, I became obsessed with the problem of sleep. *Why* couldn't I sleep? Within a week, it became the only thing I thought or cared about. I was consumed with cracking the code. I tried everything: eliminating caffeine, abstaining from naps, and wearing blue-light-filtering glasses after five in the evening. I also peppered my friends with questions about their sleep habits—this aspect of their lives was suddenly the most interesting thing about them.

But my insomnia only worsened. Every day as the sun began to set, I would feel a surge of anxiety as I anticipated the hours of tossing and turning that lay ahead. Would I ever sleep normally again? I fantasized about falling sick. (If I were hospitalized, doctors might be forced to give me a sedative that would properly knock me out.) But what exasperated me more than my exhaustion was that there appeared to be no obvious cause for my insomnia. If I hadn't been able to sleep because I was stressed over a work project or an issue with a friend, that would've been one thing, but my mind had just decided to go rogue and self-sabotage.

About a month into this experience, just as I was despairing that my insomnia might never lift, I had an unexpected shift in perspective. One Sunday morning, I walked to the farmers market in our little downtown area. Swirling in my angst, I put in my earbuds and listened to one of my favorite recordings, César Franck's Violin Sonata, performed by the violinist Ray Chen.

In the middle of the third movement, the violin introduces a stirring melody that slowly builds in intensity—it is hauntingly beautiful. As the melody played on, my heart swelled. The strings were singing. I felt myself surrender to the music, and as I did so, something within me released. It was as if a tiny needle had punctured a high-pressure balloon.

The music was, of course, not a silver bullet for my insomnia—it would be months before I reestablished my normal sleep patterns—but it did offer me a way to zoom out when I was feeling hopeless. In the weeks preceding that morning at the farmers market, I had come to see daytime as one long runway before nighttime, when I would get another chance to prove to myself that I could sleep. But, as the melody elevated me to a new place, I was able, just for a moment, to escape the mental prison I'd constructed. For the first time in a while, I felt something other than fury at my brain. I was grateful I could still be awestruck.

4

A Hole in the Heart

When Tara Sharp was growing up, there was no one she admired more than her dad, Felix. An artist by trade, he was a deeply kind man with a boundless enthusiasm for helping others. When a storm flooded their Northern California town, Felix woke up at dawn for several weeks straight to fill care packages with blankets and lunches for families who'd been displaced from their homes. He was an active member of the PTA and a volunteer art teacher. He also regularly organized charity events and food drives through the local church.

Felix's career as an artist occasionally took his family to new places, and he brought his community spirit with him wherever they went. Just weeks after moving to a fishing village in Mexico, he had already made friends with families in the area. He developed a routine of picking up Tara and her two little brothers from school and inviting their classmates to join them for a game of soccer on the beach.

"When my dad arrived at school each afternoon, I remember looking at him and thinking, 'Wow, I am so proud this guy is my dad,'" Tara said.

But her dad was also prone to sporadic verbal outbursts. One afternoon, when Tara was eight, Felix went outside to dig trenches around the perimeter of their house and clean out the gutters after a heavy rainstorm. When he came back inside, he announced to the family all that he'd done. Then, inexplicably, he began to repeat himself. Soon, he was yelling, berating Tara's mom for not sufficiently appreciating his efforts. After that experience, Tara became hyper-attuned to any signs that a transformation might be taking place within her dad. One telltale signal was that he would become irritated by things that wouldn't ordinarily matter to him. "Suddenly, the way you made your bed, which was the way you'd been making it for the last six months, was a massive problem. He'd lose his temper and start screaming at the top of his lungs," Tara said. Other times, it was the family cat that triggered his anger. Felix's response after every flare-up was the same: his cheeks would turn beet red with embarrassment, and then he'd apologize profusely and retreat to his bedroom. Tara's mom would tell Tara and her brothers that their dad was sick.

The contrast between the father she loved so dearly and the angry man who sometimes emerged without warning was hard for Tara to understand. At her young age, she did not know the full context of her dad's mental-health struggles. It would be years before she learned that when he'd been drafted to serve in the Vietnam War, his job had been to fly planes carrying the bodies of American soldiers back to the United States for burial. After every flight, he would vomit and be unable to keep food down for days. When he finally returned home from the war, he started to suffer from post-traumatic stress disorder.

Felix had one of his worst outbursts when Tara was eleven. It was New Year's Eve, and he'd taken out the special wedding china so that he and the kids could prepare appetizers in time to celebrate with Tara's mom when she returned home from work. Felix patiently taught them how to cut up slices of cheese, cucumbers, and carrots and fan them out on the platters so that they looked extra fancy. Then he went upstairs to change into more festive clothes. Tara and her brothers took the opportunity to sneak a few bites of the appetizers. When Felix came back and saw the missing pieces, he became irate. In a rage, he picked up one of the platters and threw it across the room against a cabinet, where it shattered into pieces. His eyes looked vacant. He had never come close to laying a finger on Tara or her brothers in the past, but in this moment Tara understood that this man they were looking at could seriously injure them. *And he might do it*, she thought. *Because this man is not my dad. This man is a stranger to me.*

Felix didn't hurt them—minutes after throwing the platter, he burst into tears and begged for their forgiveness. Then he retreated to his room, where he stayed, with the curtains drawn, for two weeks. Tara's mom shuttled mugs of tea and bowls of soup into the bedroom. Through closed doors, Tara could overhear her mom's hushed phone calls with a doctor. Tara knew her dad was in pain, so she made a resolution: she would love her dad so much that he wouldn't feel this pain. Her love would fix him.

Loving her dad well, in Tara's mind, meant constantly making him proud and never triggering him. She brought home only excellent report cards. She was on her best behavior at school so that she could earn "sunshine notes" from her teachers and then share these notes of praise with him. She kept her room tidy, folding her clothes in the precise way he had taught her. In her adolescent years, she rarely spoke back. She also gave him fierce hugs before bed every night and before school each morning, hoping that her affection might insulate him from his demons.

After years of burying herself in her schoolwork, Tara was awarded a full-ride scholarship to college. On the third night of her freshman orientation in Washington, D.C., she found a pay phone on campus and called home to tell her parents just how much she was enjoying school and how she'd already made a few friends. Her parents were overjoyed. Though Tara's dad wasn't much of a drinker, he insisted that they open a bottle of champagne to celebrate her achievement. Tara was touched. The three of them did a long-distance "cheers" over the phone. Before they hung up, Tara's dad told her just how proud of her he was.

The next day, when Tara called home again, her mom immediately picked up. Her tone was robotic. She asked Tara to catch the next flight home to California—there had been a family emergency. Tara spent the flight bracing herself for news about her elderly grandfather, who had recently become ill. But when she arrived home that evening, she learned that her dad had died by suicide.

Hundreds of people attended the memorial service. The community struggled to grasp how someone so kind and cheerful could end his life. For Tara, it was simply incomprehensible that this man whom she loved so deeply was suddenly gone. "When my dad died, it felt like someone had taken a knife and plunged it into my heart and then chopped it up into a million different pieces," she said. "I went to the library and looked up whether it was possible to die of a broken heart."

In the months following her dad's death, Tara moved back to California so that she could better support her mom and brothers. She kept herself feverishly busy, enrolling at Sonoma State University and petitioning the school board to let her take extra classes. She also spent every weeknight and weekend working at a local winery. Anytime she felt tears welling up, she'd call the winery and offer to work additional hours. The more she had on her plate, the less time she had to engage with her grief.

Tara also broke up with her long-term boyfriend, Jonny. She'd always assumed the two of them would get married, but now the emotional intimacy they shared terrified her. It was no longer safe to love anyone, at least not in the profound way she had loved her father. Her love for him had not fixed him—it had only destroyed her. The wisest thing to do, she felt, was to remove herself from any situation in which a person could hurt her again. "You know how there are those stop-motion videos of a butterfly coming out of its chrysalis and spreading out its wings?" Tara asked. "Emotionally, I did the reverse." As her dad had done during his bouts of illness, Tara pulled the curtains closed and withdrew.

Major changes can produce ripples across nearly every domain of life. These ripples affect our inner lives, drawing us into denial, shifting our set of possible selves, or sending us into mental spirals. But they can also travel through our social lives, distorting, straining, and sometimes even breaking our relationships. For Tara, her father's suicide indirectly led to the end of her relationship with her boyfriend and also caused many of her other relationships to shift. In the years following her dad's death, Tara made good on her commitment to keep people at arm's length. She had been close to her two little brothers, especially her brother Krishna, throughout their childhood; now they began to drift apart. When her college friends asked about her dad, Tara would tell them that he'd died by suicide but wouldn't talk about how his death had affected her. She also avoided getting emotionally close to anyone she dated.

The strain that a major change puts on our relationships can often escape our notice initially. But when we do start to register how our relationships have shifted, it can cause us to feel confused or troubled. We might wonder why we're now acting strangely around others, or why they're acting strangely around us. We may feel alienated from our closest friends or let down by them. Or maybe we are bewildered that someone who is undergoing the same change as we are is having a vastly different reaction; perhaps they want to process everything out loud, whereas we prefer to work through things internally. As we navigate these shifts, we may yearn to return to how we interacted with others before the change—the seamless communication we once shared with a spouse, or the easy humor we had with a friend.

One way of understanding why and how change can alter our relationships is through a framework called *attachment theory*, which examines how each of us forms emotional bonds with others. Attachment theory was first developed in the 1950s and '60s by the psychologists John Bowlby and Mary Ainsworth, who studied it in the context of babies forming bonds with their caregivers. But researchers have since found that the framework of attachment can also provide a useful way for us to understand our tendencies and behaviors in our adult relationships, whether with our partners, family members, friends, or acquaintances.

There are three primary attachment styles. If a person is *securely attached*, they're comfortable with emotional intimacy and believe in people's ability to love and support them; they have a fundamental feeling of safety with others. If someone is *anxiously attached*, they crave emotional intimacy but are insecure about other people's commitment to them; this can lead them to obsessively seek out reassurance, attention, and affection. If someone is *avoidantly attached*, they fear emotional intimacy altogether, just as Tara did after her father's death. They find it difficult to express their emotional needs or to trust others, and this often causes them to be overly self-reliant.

People's attachment styles can vary across their relationships. A person might, for instance, feel securely attached to their romantic partner but anxiously attached to their parents. Attachment behaviors can also vary across circumstances; research shows, for example, that stressful situations can activate more insecure behaviors. That said, in general, each of us tends to lean toward a particular attachment style, and which one we favor is a function of a complex combination of innate and environmental factors. As an example of the latter, a major change can shift our attachment style. Experiencing a betrayal or the unexpected end of a relationship or the loss of a loved one, for example, can amplify the feeling that there is safety in avoidance. By limiting our emotional attachment to others, we minimize our chances of being hurt again.

Eight years after her father's death, when Tara was twenty-six, she was invited to a friend's house for a weekend stay. There, she met Ben. He was strikingly handsome and charismatic, and Tara was smitten. By the end of the trip, they had exchanged phone numbers. A month later, they went on a first date and began a relationship. Ben was smart and worldly. He shared Tara's love of travel, and they delighted in comparing their favorite trips over dinner dates. But, above all, he made her feel comfortable. Having had a challenging childhood himself, Ben, too, was emotionally unavailable, and he would often matter-of-factly ask Tara for distance or time alone. The fact that he was this way gave her license to love him with limits. It was a good match, she thought, with walls on both sides of the relationship.

These walls made Tara feel safe. Whenever they began to come down, she instinctively put them back up. In romantic moments, she would hold Ben's gaze only briefly before looking away. Even after they got married, when everyday activities like chatting in bed or sharing a cup of coffee began to feel too intimate, Tara would excuse herself to go on a walk or to work. But no one would have been able to detect this disconnect from the outside. Tara and Ben enjoyed each other's company and were physically affectionate. They were kind and thoughtful with each other. They cofounded a small winery in Sonoma County and spent most of their waking hours together, running the business. The fissure between them existed in the silences—in what was not said, in sweet moments that came to an abrupt end.

.

After six years together, Tara and Ben began trying to start a family. Even though she'd long assumed she would be a mother someday, she needed a push from Ben. She was scared that her child, like her dad, might suddenly leave her one day. But when Tara found out that she was pregnant, she reveled in the joy of buying cute baby clothes and brainstorming names with Ben. When their daughter, Cece, was born, Tara was shocked by the intense rush of emotion that swept over her. "All of my breath left me," she said. "Everything around me stopped. I couldn't hear or see anyone else. I felt possessed by this biochemical, hormonal reaction that was impossible to tame." Cece was the most beautiful thing Tara had ever seen, and now it was Tara's job to take care of her. Tara knew that she was giving in to the very thing she'd promised herself she would resist: to love someone wholly, without guardrails. But it was irresistible. "I felt a tsunami wave of attachment," Tara said.

About a year and a half after Cece was born, Tara and Ben began planning for a second child. Tara soon got pregnant with another baby girl, but her early excitement quickly faded. Her morning sickness became so severe that she was vomiting up to twenty times a day. Meanwhile, Tara and Ben's winery suffered from declining sales. Convinced that the business was going to fail, Ben entered a state of panic. He started working around the clock and had little bandwidth to provide support at home, leaving nearly all of Cece's caregiving to Tara.

One evening, as Tara's pregnancy approached the six-month mark, she started packing for a business trip. Her nausea had largely resolved, and the winery was co-hosting a James Beard food-and-wine event in New York City. But, as she folded her clothes and placed them in her suitcase, she was overcome with exhaustion. She decided to cancel her trip and stay at home to rest. As she unpacked, she remembered that her ob-gyn had given her the option of a 3D ultrasound. Since Tara was about to turn thirty-five, her pregnancy would soon be considered high-risk. She had initially declined the appointment, but now, with her calendar newly freed up, she decided to drive down to the clinic the following morning.

The ultrasound technician was warm and chatty, asking Tara about her day and her plans for the upcoming weekend. But as she moved the wand around Tara's belly, the technician suddenly grew quiet. She began responding to Tara's questions with clipped, staccato answers. Eventually, the technician excused herself from the room.

A few minutes later, a doctor walked in and explained to Tara what the ultrasound scan had revealed: her baby had a big hole in her heart.

All at once, everything went blank for Tara. Her hands trembling, she called Ben from the exam table. It went straight to voicemail. She tried three more times and then remembered that he was at the vineyard, which had no cell service. A nurse gently escorted Tara to a small room where a genetic counselor asked her if she had any family history of heart disease. Tara racked her brain. Her grandfather had had heart attacks, but he'd had an unhealthy lifestyle. Then it hit her: her aunt Kay had recently passed away from a heart condition. Tara had never learned what her aunt's condition was called, so she called her mom, Heather, and put her on speakerphone.

"Hi, Mom . . . something is wrong with the baby's heart," Tara let out weakly. "They're asking if there's any history of heart disease in our family, and I thought of Auntie Kay." Heather knew what Tara was referring to, but she also didn't know the condition's name. She excused herself to fetch a folder filled with the relevant medical information. When she returned, she carefully and slowly read the words: "Tetralogy of Fallot."

Tara saw the blood drain from the genetic counselor's face. Tetralogy of Fallot was a rare and serious congenital condition that involved multiple defects in the heart. Since the condition often runs in families, the counselor asked Heather if other members of their family had had the same issue.

"Well, my other sister who lived only for a short time—she had it, too," Heather answered tightly. The counselor probed further and asked if there were any other relatives affected. Heather took a deep breath. She then shared that some dozen members of Tara's extended family had had the condition, an unprecedented number in the world of cardiology. In fact, unbeknownst to Tara, her family had served as a fascinating case study for cardiologists, who had analyzed the prevalence of the heart condition in Tara's lineage dating back to the early 1900s—they'd even published their findings in a renowned medical journal. As far as Heather knew, Auntie Kay was the only family member born with the condition who had survived into adulthood. Heather had been advised by her primary-care doctor not to tell any of her children about the condition. He believed it would cause needless stress: since Tara and her brothers had all been born healthy, the risk of their having offspring with the condition had seemed small.

Tara was in shock. The clinic's doctor advised termination of the pregnancy while it still fell within California's legal abortion window. Tara then asked a friend to go find Ben at the vineyard and have him drive to the clinic right away. By the time Ben arrived, Tara had fallen into a stupor and the doctor had to fill him in on everything.

Over the next twenty-four hours, Tara and Ben researched the condition to better understand their options. They tracked down a heart surgeon in Northern California with expertise on the condition and were squeezed in for a last-minute appointment. The surgeon told them that he could perform a high-risk experimental surgery on the baby soon after her birth that had a 30 percent chance of success. If that surgery went well, then the baby would require at least one additional high-risk surgery when she was older. The surgeon told Tara that she would effectively be delivering a terminally ill baby.

Tara and Ben were paralyzed by the magnitude of the decision before them, and by how quickly they'd need to make it. Tara in particular felt she was in no position to decide anything at all, given her emotional state. After some discussion, they both agreed that the heart surgeon, the one who would have to perform the experimental surgery on their baby, should make the decision for them.

"Please let me try," the doctor said.

With that, Tara and Ben chose to move forward with the pregnancy. Tara experienced a flurry of conflicting emotions as she felt the unborn child within her transform from a baby girl into a patient. She also felt herself transform from an expectant mom into a caregiver. In the weeks that followed, instead of dreaming about first giggles and tiny fingers and toes, she aggressively pushed thoughts of her pregnancy from her mind, at times even fooling herself into believing she wasn't pregnant. When people commented on her growing belly, she would redirect the conversation toward a sweet or funny story about Cece. Tara accepted a new, demanding job, not only because it was precarious for her family to depend entirely on the winery for their income, but also because the work helped distract her from her anxiety. She hid Cece's favorite article of clothing, her "Big Sister" T-shirt, on the top shelf of a closet. And, before falling asleep at night, Tara would rehearse the speech she'd one day have to give Cece about what had happened to her baby sister.

One evening, about four weeks before her scheduled C-section, Tara began to feel short of breath and called the doctor. After hearing her symptoms, he arranged for an emergency helicopter ride to the hospital where the baby's open-heart surgery would be performed. As the nurses loaded Tara into the helicopter, the technicians strapped her legs together and told her that if she had contractions, she should try her hardest not to push. Tara looked out of the helicopter window and saw that the moon was full and bright. Despite the months of telling herself not to get attached to the baby inside her, she now found herself looking down at her belly and whispering, "Hold on, little girl. Just hold on a bit longer, okay?"

Two hours later, Tara delivered Ellie. The doctors wrapped Ellie in a hospital blanket, and though Tara could see only her tiny nose and the top of her lip poking out, she again thought that this daughter of hers was the most beautiful thing she had ever seen. Tara was terrified by the potential of connecting with her newborn, but this time she wasn't given a chance to bond. Ellie was whisked away to the neonatal intensive care unit. Tara was not allowed to hold her even briefly. The rush of attachment that Tara had felt after Cece's birth never came.

●

Five days after she was born, Ellie was wheeled from the NICU into the operating room for open-heart surgery. Tara was more scared than she'd ever been. "Here I was, actively handing my sick but *alive* child over to doctors, knowing full well she had a good chance of dying," she said. Desperate to find something positive to hold on to, she reminded herself that she and Ben would at least get some resolution about Ellie's fate.

But when the surgeons inspected Ellie's heart, they discovered that the situation was far worse than they had expected. Although they could make some small surgical improvements, they would need to delay the bulk of the surgery until Ellie was at least six months old and could tolerate a highly complex fourteen-hour procedure. The procedure would involve connecting Ellie to a heart-bypass machine while surgeons mended the hole and reconstructed a pulmonary artery and a valve using tissue from a donor. *Six months*, Tara thought. *Six months of complete torture*. Even though she felt a strong pang of guilt at the mere idea, she couldn't help but wonder whether there was an option to leave Ellie under the care of hospital staff until then. Maybe they could just call her once Ellie was in the clear?

A few days later, Tara and Ben brought Ellie home. Ellie's tiny body was blue and weak, and because she didn't have the strength to nurse or bottle-feed, she had to eat via a feeding tube. Tara and Ben grew only more distant from each other in the weeks that followed. Ben was struggling with his own grief, collapsing under the weight of Ellie's precarious health and the stress of keeping their small winery afloat. He began to retreat further into himself, barely speaking or showing any emotion. He also started exerting obsessive control over other aspects of his life, like adhering to a militant diet and exercise plan. He insisted that the dishwasher be stacked and unloaded in a certain way, that the kitchen counters be kept pristine, and that the temperature of the house be set to sixty-seven degrees. When Tara folded the laundry, Ben would refold everything to his liking. He would get mad when he saw Cece's toys in the living room instead of in her bedroom. "You know she's just a kid, right, Ben?" Tara bristled. But she had no energy to fight him. She was frustrated that it felt like she was always failing him. Soon, she grew numb to his prob-lems. One afternoon, when he told her that he'd just had a fight with his mom, Tara replied that he would need to discuss it with someone else. She simply couldn't make space for his issues.

What had once been an emotional gap between Tara and Ben had grown into a chasm. They hardly felt like a couple anymore, coming together only to schedule doctor's appointments, pay medical bills, and co-parent their toddler and their terminally ill baby. Tara knew that Ben was the sole person who could truly understand what she was going through, and vice versa. But for this very reason, they couldn't tolerate each other's presence. It was better to spend time with people who could distract them from Ellie's situation. "Anytime I was around Ben, I would begin to cry, and so would he," Tara said. "So it was just easier to avoid interacting."

She also began to feel increasingly disconnected from her extended community. Before Ellie's birth, Tara was already becoming alien-ated from other moms. Whenever she entered the room at her prenatal-yoga class, a tense silence would fill the air, as conversations about baby names and nursery decorations came to a halt. Soon, the women stopped inviting her out to tea or for walks. When her friends suggested that they throw Tara a baby shower, she resisted; baby showers were supposed to be fun and light affairs.

These dynamics only worsened after Ellie was born. Tara's usually lively family members were now eerily quiet at gatherings, never ex-actly sure what to say or how to behave around her. She and her brother Krishna had already grown apart following their dad's death, and he now drifted even further away, rarely calling, visiting, or offering Tara any support. Many of Tara's friends treated her as fragile; they avoided sharing their everyday problems with her lest they add to her burden or be seen as comparing their situations to hers. When a coworker heard the news of Ellie's condition, she expressed her condolences to Tara and then never again acknowledged Ellie's existence. "It was as if everyone was holding their breath, waiting for the worst possible news," Tara said.

It became harder and harder for Tara to get out of bed in the morning. She hardly ate and spent her days crying. She had trouble sleeping because she was worried that at any moment Ellie might stop breathing. Tara was so depleted that she wondered if she might be dying.

·

Tara knew she needed professional help. She saw a psychiatrist, who diagnosed her with postpartum depression and prescribed her antidepressants. Tara began counting down the days until the six-month mark, when Ellie would finally have her surgery, and when Tara would finally know whether it was safe to love her.

Tara was ashamed that she was withholding love from Ellie. She choked out the words "I love you" to her, if only so that she could feel like she'd checked one of the most basic boxes of motherhood. "I just felt so terrible. Like, here's this sweet, innocent little baby who, through no fault of her own, has this health issue," Tara said. "And then here I am, this mother who is absolutely terrified to love her." Tara was exhausted from the effort it was taking to maintain this emotional gulf. When her guilt would overwhelm her, Tara would ask Ben or her mom to help out. Would they mind singing a lullaby or snuggling with Ellie, while Tara took care of Cece? Could they read Ellie a bedtime story? "I need you to love Ellie more right now," Tara told them. "Because I know I can't."

By the time Ellie was three months old, Tara was driving her to and from the hospital three times a week so that the cardiologists could check her vitals and her heart health. Ellie was getting stronger by the day, and, actually, so was Tara. The antidepressants had taken full effect, and Tara was exercising and meditating on a regular basis. She began reclaiming parts of herself, bit by bit, and rediscovered the joy in small things: the feeling of the sun on her face, the zing of the lemon in her salad dressing, the warmth of a cuddle with her dog. One afternoon, a friend came over for tea, and she and Tara chatted about their favorite running shoes. It was refreshing for Tara to lose herself in such an ordinary conversation. On the morning of Ellie's next hospital visit, Tara retired her sweatpants in favor of a nice pair of jeans and a pretty sweater.

As she drove back home from the appointment and pulled into the garage, Tara caught a glimpse of Ellie in the rearview mirror. Ellie's feeding tube had been removed, and with fewer medical implements plastered to her daughter's face, Tara could see that Ellie's cheeks had filled out and were more pink than blue.

Tara parked the car and opened the back door to grab Ellie's diaper bag. "Hi, sweetheart!" Tara said. Ellie cooed and smiled in her car seat, turning toward the sound of Tara's voice and staring directly into her eyes. Tara stared back. She was stunned by Ellie's beauty.

Tara set down the diaper bag. Then she staggered and collapsed, her knees falling onto the cold concrete of the garage floor. She let out heaving sobs, surrendering to her daughter's presence. "Suddenly, it just became so clear to me that I wanted to love Ellie, even if it meant getting hurt," Tara said, "because the fear of my loving her was completely depleting me."

After several minutes, Tara found the strength to stand up again and lift Ellie from her car seat. For the first time, she allowed herself to study her daughter, marveling at her tiny fingers and her sparkling, bright eyes.

"Ellie," Tara whispered, drawing out each syllable. "Ellie, I love you."

Tara knew that things could end catastrophically—she and Ben might still lose their daughter. It made sense for Tara to continue guarding herself, but withholding her love from Ellie had become unsustainable. After her breakdown in the garage, Tara started taking small steps to cultivate a relationship with her baby. She cradled Ellie in the living-room rocking chair, staring into her eyes for a few seconds at a time. When Tara started to feel scared by her growing attachment, she'd stop and try again. When she went to the store to buy clothes for Ellie, she gave herself permission to enjoy just how cute the little outfits were. Bedtime went from a routine activity to a series of sweet interactions between them. "It was terrifying at first," Tara said.

"But I allowed myself to start investing in the small moments we shared together. I slowly let myself fall fully in love with her."

When Ellie turned six months old and it was finally time for her big surgery, the doctors had a difficult time getting Tara to leave her daughter's side in the operating room. She kept kissing Ellie and telling her how much she loved her. During Ellie's initial surgery as a newborn, Tara had mentally checked out; this time, she was completely present.

Nearly fourteen hours later, when the heart surgeon emerged from the operating room, he had remarkable news for Tara and Ben: the surgery had been successful, and Ellie was recovering well. Although she would require another big open-heart surgery at the age of seven before doctors could officially remove her "terminally ill" label, everyone could at least rest easy knowing that Ellie had made it past this major obstacle.

By now, Tara had fallen hopelessly in love with Ellie, and there was no turning back, regardless of what the future held. "The only thing I can liken it to is being a little kid who is scared to jump off the diving board," Tara said. "As you're about to make the plunge, you think, 'This is really scary. I could die. Actually, I am going to die. This is definitely going to kill me.' And then you land in the swimming pool, and you get a headful of chlorinated water up your nose, and it definitely hurts like hell. But you didn't die. And then . . . you feel a little exhilarated."

Tara describes the years following Ellie's open-heart surgery at six months old as some of the happiest of her life. Despite all the unknowns at the time, Tara remained intentional about embracing her love for Ellie. She remembers one sunny afternoon, just months after the surgery, when she took Ellie and Cece on a walk in the countryside, eventually stumbling upon a beautiful apple orchard. When they spotted a horse nearby, both girls squealed with joy. Tara fed the horse an apple, and Ellie laughed and laughed and laughed. Later in the day, Tara pulled Ellie out of her stroller so that she could crawl in the park. By the end of the outing, Ellie had grass stains all over her pants. Tara beamed. "I was so happy for the littlest things," she said. "How lucky were we, for Ellie to have this life where she could move around and play in the grass?"

Ellie's surgery at the age of seven was a success. She will need one more surgery, around the age of twenty, when her heart outgrows the size of its donor parts, but the doctors are optimistic that this operation will be straightforward; they expect that she will live a long, full life. Today, Ellie is a healthy, thriving teenager. Gentle and affectionate, she plays on the school's JV basketball team (Ben is the assistant coach), loves cooking and baking with Tara and Cece, and enjoys snuggling with their dog.

Since that moment with Ellie in the garage, Tara, with the help of a therapist, has undertaken years of emotional work to overcome her fear of attachment. That work has had positive effects on many of her relationships. She ended up having a candid conversation with Krishna about how he'd disappointed her during Ellie's first big surgery. He apologized and told her that he had been overwhelmed by the situation and had simply shut down. During this talk, Tara summoned up the courage to be more explicit with him about the kind of support she needed. When Ellie had her second big surgery, at age seven, Krishna visited Tara, organized meals, and sent regular updates about Ellie to their extended family. "He did everything I asked, and more," Tara said.

Tara also began investing in people she'd known for a long time but had hesitated to confide in. One of them was her friend Claire, whom she'd met years earlier at a winery event. As their friendship solidified, Tara would call Claire whenever she was scared or sad, and Claire would listen while Tara sobbed. Some calls would end with Tara having spoken no words at all. They texted daily and cooked together. Claire would often stop by Tara's house to clean up her bedroom, fold laundry, or play with Cece and Ellie. Years earlier, Tara could not have imagined depending on someone for such intense emotional support. "Claire was almost like a mom to me during that period of time," Tara said. "It was beautiful to have the safety of someone to go to."

Over the years, Tara's relationship with Claire gave her the confidence to expand her circle of support and to build what she now describes as a sisterhood. Her friends sat by her side whenever Ellie was in the hospital and would often show up at her doorstep with food. They celebrated Ellie's victories and cried during her setbacks. "I had believed for so long that keeping my fear inside of me would keep it controlled," Tara said. "What I actually found is that, once I started talking about it with my friends, my fear had a lot less power over me."

As a result of Tara's newfound vulnerability, her friends began confiding in her too. One of them, Steph, opened up to Tara about her struggles raising a young daughter with type 1 diabetes. Sometimes Steph and Tara would simply sit together on a park bench holding hands as they watched their kids play. "It was just these small acts of intimacy," Tara said. When Claire's house burned down in a California wildfire, Tara helped with everything from logistics to emotional support; she'd also listen to Claire cry on the phone, just as Claire had once done for her.

·

When change upends our lives, our first response may be to adopt a narrow view of our situation—whether by denying its reality, foreclosing on possible selves, or ruminating. After her father's death, Tara closed herself off and vowed never to become attached to others again. But change doesn't have to limit us; it can also present an opportunity to expand our lives in ways that we may not have thought possible. Eventually, Olivia, as she navigated being locked in, Dwayne, as he grappled with a prison sentence, and Matt, as he reckoned with the consequences of his on-air panic attack, all found ways to reimagine themselves within the constraints of their new circumstances. For Tara, a second major change—having a child with a serious health condition—ultimately offered her a chance to examine the relational patterns she had developed after losing her dad. She learned that she didn't have to limit herself as she had for years; there was another path available to her, one full of rich and rewarding relationships. Tara's story invites us to think more expansively about what a life disruption can offer us. What if we saw change as a chance to reconsider how we relate to others?

In Tara's case, she was inspired to try to shift her attachment style. Indeed, recent research shows that attachment styles are far more malleable than psychologists once thought—new life experiences can continually reshape them. As the journalist Faith Hill writes in *The Atlantic*, "The common misconception is that one's style is set in stone during childhood, determined by connections with early caregivers, and doomed to play out in every relationship thereafter." But it turns out that the association between a person's early experiences and their adult attachment style is weak. "Attachment orientation is complex," Hill writes. "It's an ongoing interaction between the external world and your internal one, between your circumstances and your interpretation of them."

What this means is that, like Tara, we can take active, deliberate steps to move in the direction of a more secure orientation. Just as negative past experiences might have pushed you toward insecure attachments, positive experiences—with people who are reliable, and who make you feel comfortable and safe—can push you toward secure ones. You don't even have to seek out new experiences if you want to initiate a shift to a more secure attachment style: research shows that it is effective to simply mine your past for examples of times when people in your life showed up for you, cared for you, or protected you. In one study that was conducted over a four-month period, people who spent time each week reflecting on past secure interactions experienced significant decreases in their attachment anxiety.

Roughly a decade after Ellie was born, Tara and Ben decided that it did not make sense for them to stay married. They were able to reach this conclusion together because, for the first time, they were willing to have difficult conversations in which they talked openly about the long-standing problems in their relationship. "When Ben and I met each other twenty years ago, we were building a thing together. What we both realized over time is that what we were building was a sandcastle that couldn't withstand the pressure of all the changes we had to confront as a couple," Tara said.

But, they thought, maybe they could rebuild *something* together, something that did not involve the expectations of a marriage. "We kind of looked at each other and said, 'I respect you more than ever. I appreciate you more than ever. I want to be an important person in your life, and for you to be the same in my life. So let's build a different type of castle together.'"

Initially, Tara thought that a divorce might "ruin her"; she was terrified of being left alone again. But having built such a supportive community, she was more empowered to take the leap. Since finalizing their divorce, Tara and Ben have developed a friendship that is stronger than it's ever been. When Tara recently experienced a major professional setback, she was transparent with Ben about her disappointment, and he was a source of support for her.

Today, Tara and Ben live in houses just blocks apart. They spend holidays together as a family and have regular dinners. During one of my conversations with Tara, Ellie and Ben were assembling an IKEA desk for Ellie's bedroom. Tara, Cece, and Ellie were planning to cook dinner together later on and bake chocolate chip cookies for dessert. It was inspiring to see the beautiful life Tara had built for herself, one that seemed to brim with love.

Tara still thinks about her dad often. "A huge part of me shut down when he died," she said. "For decades, I missed my dad so much. I would feel a physical pain in my chest every time I thought of him. But my experience with Ellie—it opened me back up. I don't feel that same kind of pain anymore." When life throws an unexpected challenge Tara's way and she finds herself withdrawing again, she remembers her commitment: "Do I want to keep living my life in this incredibly guarded, fearful way, or do I want to live openly, even if it carries the cost of being crushed? For as long as it's possible, I want to choose the latter."

The Blank Slate

Hours before the sun rose, Ingrid Rojas Contreras, along with her parents and her little sister, stuffed the trunk of their car with suitcases and set off on the road for their annual vacation. The fourteen-hour drive from Bogotá to Ingrid's maternal grandmother's house, which was nestled in a rural village at the foot of the Colombian Andes, would be a treacherous one. It was the early 1990s, and the country roiled with conflict as the government, paramilitary organizations, and crime syndicates, including Pablo Escobar's Medellín Cartel, struggled for power. The volatile political situation made everyday life for Colombians perilous. Resistance groups were planting bombs in cars, buildings, and even people's homes. Kidnappings were commonplace as well; Ingrid's family alone had received dozens of threats over the years.

In the days leading up to the long drive, Ingrid's father did his usual scan of the local newspaper to identify any guerrilla fighters or ongoing conflicts that they should try to avoid along the way. Still, they were stopped at several military checkpoints by soldiers who searched their car for illegal items and questioned Ingrid's father about his political allegiances. When Ingrid's family finally arrived at her grandmother's house, it was difficult to relax and recover. The air was stiflingly hot, and there was no electricity or running water due to a recent drought in the area.

But eight-year-old Ingrid didn't mind the stress of the day's travel or the lack of creature comforts. She rejoiced in these gatherings with her extended family. Their evenings together would always start off festive, with dancing and singing in the backyard garden to the cumbia music that played on the radio. As soon as it became clear, though, that Ingrid's mom, Sojaila, was ready to share her first story of the night, the focus of the gathering would shift. This night was no exception. An expectant silence filled the air as the family oriented their chairs toward Sojaila. The other children had nodded off hours ago, but Ingrid fought back her yawns; she always insisted on staying up for the family's storytelling. Everyone was enraptured, but Ingrid especially so.

Some of Sojaila's stories were reminiscent of those told by other Colombian families with rural backgrounds—what life was like in the mountains or how, when Sojaila was a little girl and food was scarce, she was sent to a nearby farm to try to bribe another family's cow to walk a full mile home with her. But then there were the tales few others could tell: stories about her family's magical powers. Ingrid's grandfather—Sojaila's father—had been a *curandero*, a traditional healer who used herbal medicines and spiritual rituals passed down through generations to treat physical and psychological ailments. It was said that he could predict the future, speak with spirits, and direct the movement of rain clouds to help farmers grow their crops. One of Sojaila's stories recounted how, when she was nine years old, a father and his young son appeared at her family's doorstep. The boy had gone through a traumatic experience and was refusing to eat. Unable to afford a hospital visit, the father had brought his son to see Sojaila's dad, who prepared special broths for the boy. Sojaila's dad then instructed Sojaila to sit at the boy's bedside throughout the night and gently talk to him about the bright future she envisioned for him. The next day, the boy's father came back to the house with the gift of a chicken and with tears of gratitude streaming down his face. His son had begun to eat again.

Sojaila, too, was a curandera; she believed she could see ghosts and exist in two places at once. In Bogotá, she ran a small word-of-mouth business out of the attic of her home, where she helped people from the community with their personal troubles. After school each day, Ingrid would rush home to eavesdrop on her mom's sessions with clients. Ingrid was by nature a philosophical child who loved peppering her parents with questions about the meaning of life; learning about her family's healing rituals fed her curiosity. Ingrid remembers one woman who'd recently lost custody of her child to her abusive ex-husband. Sojaila whispered prayers into a bowl of water and then handed the water to the woman to drink. The woman left the attic with a newfound serenity. Ingrid often thought about how lucky she was to have been born into a family of curanderos who carried such rich spiritual traditions.

But while Indigenous beliefs like these might have been common in the village that Sojaila had grown up in, they were unusual in modern Bogotá. City dwellers saw curanderos as uncivilized and ignorant. They hurled insults at Sojaila, spat in her face, and harassed her. Others took out their anger on Ingrid's family by excluding them from social gatherings and conspiring to get Ingrid's dad fired from his job. Over time, Sojaila began using more palatable Western terms to describe her work, like "fortune teller" and "someone with an ability to see."

One afternoon, Ingrid told her mom a piece of gossip she'd heard from a friend at school, and Sojaila was reminded how readily children repeat what they hear. She sat Ingrid down and gave her a strict admonition: Ingrid was *never* to share her family's stories with anyone outside of their family. These stories were likely to be met with scorn and ridicule or, worse yet, violence. This was why, perhaps, those magical stories came out only late at night, when Ingrid's family was tucked away in the safety of her grandmother's home. Taking in her mom's warning, Ingrid nodded. Her family's stories weren't merely stories. They were secrets to be kept.

When Ingrid was nineteen, she immigrated to the United States to study journalism and creative writing at a liberal arts college in Chicago. Her fascination with stories had persisted into adulthood, and she longed for a job that would allow her to tell other people's stories.

Ingrid found the novelty of life in Chicago exhilarating. She was taken by the charm of the big city and found the cold weather shocking in its intensity. Having learned English in secondary school, she was able to quickly build a new group of friends. She also began dating an artist named Jeremiah. But, though she enjoyed soaking in the culture around her, she became increasingly guarded about sharing her family's culture with her new community. "I existed in a constant state of withholding," Ingrid said. Jeremiah was frustrated that she so rarely opened up to him about her past. Her friends came to know her as the "inscrutable one." "I didn't want to be examined or gawked at, and so I just chose to stay silent on those parts of myself," she said. "Even the smallest thing about my family, I just wouldn't be able to share it. I was a small percentage of myself."

In a freshman writing class, Ingrid drafted the first pages of what she thought could become a memoir. She figured that if she was ever going to share her family's heritage with others, it'd be easier to do it with a bunch of strangers than with her close friends. But when she showed her writing to her classmates and presented it as nonfiction, they balked, suggesting that it was just one big tall tale. Then they lectured her about the difference between fiction and nonfiction. Ingrid put the memoir aside and started writing a novel instead. Her mom had been right—her family's stories were not meant to be shared.

Over time, Ingrid's identity split into two. There was the American version of herself, who was rapidly assimilating to the wide, paved streets of Chicago and picking up new mannerisms, such as weaving the word "like" into her speech. And then there was the Colombian version, who thought of the winding dirt roads back home whenever she spoke in Spanish on the phone with her mom. "I was someone in English, and then I was someone else entirely in Spanish," Ingrid recalled. "And people knew only one or the other. I started to feel as though no one in the world knew me as one whole."

·

In her first few years out of college, Ingrid worked as a freelance Spanish-English translator for magazines and newspapers. She'd taken up the gig to pay the bills as she tried to carve out a life as a writer. Late one afternoon, she took a short break from writing her novel and hopped onto her road bike to pick up a dress she'd dropped off with a tailor. She sped down the busy city streets, hoping to reach the shop before it closed for the day.

The next thing Ingrid knew, she was on the ground, her head searing with pain. The sound of her skull hitting the pavement just a moment earlier registered in her consciousness. She remained splayed on the road as cars whizzed by and the sounds of honking horns filled her ears. As she lay there, she was struck by a strange sense that she was far lighter than before—unburdened in some way, freed of something heavy.

Ingrid sat up in a daze and looked around. An older man with a scruffy beard stood above her, offering her his hand. She managed to stand up without his assistance. *I guess I must be fine,* she thought. She tried to piece together what had happened. Clearly she had fallen, because why else would she have ended up on the street? Behind her, she spotted an open car door. There was a bicycle on the ground, a foot or so away from her. Things started to click into place: *I must have been biking when I hit an open car door.*

Ingrid lifted her bike off the road and clambered onto its seat. The bearded man again came over and straightened out the handlebars, which had been twisted in the crash. Ingrid thanked him and then pedaled forward a block. She biked past the streets at the next intersection—but she didn't recognize their names. She biked a block farther. Still no recognition. It occurred to her that she didn't even know what city she was in. She slowed down and parked her bike on a street corner.

Then it hit her all at once: she did not know who she was or where she was from.

I've lost my memories, Ingrid realized.

Strangely, she was not alarmed. She glanced down and saw that she had a messenger bag slung across her chest. It might contain clues about who she was.

But then Ingrid was struck by another thought. Maybe she didn't *want* to recover her memories—not quite yet, anyway. It was a peculiar idea, but she found the sensation of emptiness, of her mind being a blank slate, euphoric. She was suddenly certain about what to do next: she would throw away her messenger bag.

But, as Ingrid walked over to a nearby trash can, she caught a glimpse of her reflection in the glass exterior of a building. Her features struck her as South American, or maybe Middle Eastern? She had been so ready to throw out her bag just moments before, but now, as she stared at her reflection, she wondered about the people who cared about her. She didn't know what kind of family she came from—what if it was a bad one? In that case, perhaps she should just throw away the bag. But what if it was a good family? Ingrid would have to find her way back to them and reassure them that she was okay.

She opened the messenger bag. There was a journal filled with pages of writing that she assumed must be hers, even though she couldn't identify the handwriting. Then she found a cell phone, which she instinctively knew how to use. She decided that she should probably call someone and let them know what had happened. She pulled up the list of her recent calls—the last person she'd called was someone named Paul. When he picked up, she explained that she'd been in a biking accident and couldn't remember basic facts about her life. Paul, eager to reassure her, began jogging her memory: Ingrid lived in Chicago with her boyfriend, Jeremiah; she had a sister to whom he, Paul, was engaged.

Then, for reasons Ingrid could not fully understand, she suddenly felt it was imperative to hide the full extent of her amnesia from her loved ones. She was continuing to marvel at her current mental state, and she didn't want anything, or anyone, to break the spell. She began insisting to Paul that she actually *did* know all of these facts—it was just the adrenaline that was preventing her from thinking clearly. But Paul nevertheless urged her to call Jeremiah so that he could take her to a doctor right away.

As Jeremiah rushed to the scene, Ingrid began skimming her journal, hoping she could learn more about herself so that Jeremiah would not be too alarmed by her memory loss. When she glanced up from the journal about ten minutes later, a worried-looking man was hurriedly getting off his bike and running to embrace her. She couldn't recognize his face, and yet, as her head found a place in the nook of his chest, her body registered it as familiar. But so much was missing, she could tell. Her memories—of this person she was holding, of her past—were gone.

The ER doctor ordered a head X-ray for Ingrid. As she lay in her hospital bed awaiting the results, she reflected on what had happened that afternoon. The sense of euphoria she'd encountered after the accident—right after she'd lost her memories—was still with her. "I felt like a ball of energy, like I was suddenly new and untouched by experiences or time," she said. "You kind of become old to yourself, and now I was alive to the world in a way that was different than before. There was this feeling of infinite possibility, that I could create my world from scratch."

The doctor diagnosed Ingrid with a concussion, but what he did not detect during his short evaluation of her was that she had developed retrograde amnesia, a condition in which people lose existing memories but are still able to form new ones. Retrograde amnesia typically involves forgetting facts rather than skills, like how to ride a bike or how to read and write. It doesn't affect one's personality, judgment, intelligence, awareness, or attention span. The degree of memory loss can vary widely. Some people lose all of their past memories, whereas others lose memories about specific topics or from certain time periods. How long it takes for people to recover their memories, and the extent to which they do, also varies.

The doctor instructed Ingrid to go home and rest as much as possible in order for her brain to heal. As Jeremiah brought Ingrid back to her apartment, she doubled down on her earlier conviction. She wanted to hold on to this freeing, singular state of mind for as long as she could. She would continue to try to hide the full extent of her memory loss from Jeremiah and her friends. That way they wouldn't intervene and help her recover her memories.

The next morning, Jeremiah quickly checked in on Ingrid before heading to work. He'd been pulling twelve-hour days for the past few months, as he was enrolled in art school full time and working shifts at a coffee shop. He fretted about being away from Ingrid, but she was secretly grateful for the time alone, because it meant that she could explore this curious mental state without any distraction. She pulled out her notepad and began to jot down some existential questions for herself. Among them was one in particular that had her spellbound: What did it mean that she'd lost so many of her memories but was this *happy*?

In the days that followed, Ingrid covered up every mirror in her apartment with bedsheets. Any glance at her reflection might inadvertently bring back some of her memories. She also did her best to avoid prolonged interactions with Jeremiah. The doctor had helped her out here, giving her clear instructions to spend her days in a dark room with the blinds closed and with minimal stimulation. By the time Jeremiah came over to her apartment each night, she'd either pretend to be asleep or say that she was too tired to talk. She somehow managed to conceal from him just how much of her memory she'd lost, in large part because she'd always been something of an enigma. "Ingrid's ability to be unread by people in general was practically her most notable quality," Jeremiah said.

But as each week passed, memories began rushing back to Ingrid, materializing in the form of intrusive thoughts, coming in chaotically and out of order. They sometimes appeared as fleeting snapshots of scenes: laughing with her friends at a bar, trudging through the snow, listening to a piece of music. After each full night of sleep, she would wake up remembering more and more about her life—details about her childhood friends, or about the violence and fear she'd faced in Colombia. Whenever a specific memory came back, she intentionally kept it at arm's length to avoid having it trigger other memories. "I had a feeling that amnesia and not having a self was one of the most important things that could happen to me," she said, "and so I wanted to stay in that state for as long as possible."

About seven weeks after her accident, an image came back to Ingrid in a flash: her mom holding tarot cards. Ingrid's family history suddenly rushed back to her: *My mom said that she could see ghosts and be in two places at once. My grandfather was a curandero—people used to say he could move clouds.* Although Ingrid found it overwhelming to recall so much at once, she soon discovered that these memories of her family felt different from her previously restored memories—the ones that she had wanted to avoid recalling. These memories filled her with wonder and a strong nostalgia for home.

"Did I ever tell you about my grandfather?" Ingrid asked Jeremiah that evening. "He was a spiritual healer . . ." Jeremiah listened attentively as she shared stories of water blessings, of palm readings, of predicting the future. He had never seen her this joyful or animated when talking about her past.

"Why in the world have you never told me these delightful stories before, Ingrid?" Jeremiah asked.

Ingrid wasn't sure. All she knew was that she had to share these stories—they were simply too charming. "Did I ever tell you . . . ?" she'd begin, to any friends who would listen. One evening a few days later, Ingrid and Jeremiah hosted a small dinner party, and Ingrid regaled her guests with stories, even showing them how to perform Sojaila's water ritual. Her friends were enchanted. Like Jeremiah, they wondered why she had never opened up about any of this before. Ingrid herself was equally bewildered. Why *hadn't* she?

An hour into the dinner party, though, an image of Sojaila, her face disapproving, flashed in Ingrid's mind. Ingrid was overcome by the realization that she had done something terribly wrong. She abruptly stopped chatting with her guests and excused herself to the bathroom. That's when a new memory came rushing back: *I'm not supposed to share these stories.*

As Ingrid stood in front of the bathroom mirror, another memory—this time, one of an emotion—resurfaced: *shame.* She remembered why she had guarded this part of her life so closely. *I am ashamed,* she thought. *My family's heritage is shameful.*

But as her reflection stared back, Ingrid discovered something curious: the shame she was suddenly aware of felt entirely intellectual. It was a concept she understood, but it was *only* that—it wasn't accompanied by any negative feelings of heaviness. Maybe that's why she had felt so free after her accident: the burden of her shame had been lifted. Her heart still racing, she wondered why she had ever felt the need to hide her family history. "Though I could recall the shape and weight of this shame," she would later write, "the sting of it was gone."

Ingrid realized that her mother had never once suggested that she, Sojaila, was ashamed of their family's heritage. In fact, it was quite the opposite. Sojaila was proud of how she had been able to use her rituals to help people heal. Perhaps her admonition to Ingrid had been entirely practical, a cautionary word to protect Ingrid from the scorn and potential violence of those who didn't understand. Perhaps it was *Ingrid* who had subconsciously added on a layer of interpretation. "If you're told you can't share things with other people because they'll judge you," she said, "you can start to believe there is something inherently wrong with the thing that you're hiding."

Ingrid fixed her hair in the mirror and returned to the dinner table. For so long, she had been saddled by the weight of keeping her family's stories hidden inside her. But now her amnesia had wiped the slate clean and given her an exhilarating sense of freedom.

Ingrid smiled mischievously at her guests. "Did I ever tell you about the time my grandpa . . . ?"

•

As we grow up, our brains absorb information and then work to identify patterns, draw inferences, weave together stories, and make sense of our environment. This information comes from all kinds of sources, including popular culture, teachers, parents, caregivers, friends, and classmates. We might come to believe that expressing sadness is a sign of weakness, or that we're good at some things but not others, or that success is defined in a specific way. We might internalize messages about what it means to be a good person, or about what being conventionally masculine or feminine entails, or that it's important to have a certain type of body. These beliefs can also be about our families, and our place within them. Perhaps we've been led to believe that we must preserve certain traditions, or that we should never question our parents, or that it is our duty to protect our younger siblings even into adulthood.

What if you woke up one day and discovered that all those beliefs had vanished? At first, you might feel a sense of disorientation, maybe even grief for the mental structures you'd constructed: your frames of reference, your long-held values, the foundation upon which you built your life and your relationships. But, like Ingrid, you might also experience a kind of freedom. You would be given an opportunity to establish your beliefs anew, without the constellation of anchors, intuitions, and biases you've accumulated in the course of your life.

Just as a change can give us an opportunity to reimagine our relationships with others, it can also prompt us to challenge beliefs that have long crystallized. In this way, a significant change can offer us a reset similar to what Ingrid experienced. Change naturally jostles our belief tapestry, loosening the threads ever so slightly. We are given an opening through which to examine faulty ideas or mistaken assumptions that we'd never thought to interrogate. A change in our lives can be an invitation to ask ourselves: Who could I be without these beliefs?

Changing our beliefs about anything can be hard. Our beliefs are embedded in the stories we tell ourselves about who we are, which the psychologist Dan McAdams refers to as our *narrative identity*. This narrative helps us make sense of the messy and complicated world around us, and allows us to find purpose and direction within it. Because we crave consistency and unity in this narrative, modifying a single thread of belief in the tapestry—one that may be deeply entangled with many other beliefs—can be a disorienting process, one that we're reluctant to initiate. This can be especially true of beliefs we formed in childhood, which served as the basis upon which we've processed every subsequent piece of information.

Take the example of Brad Snyder, who built a strong narrative identity around his military service. Brad grew up in a military family, and he aspired to follow in the footsteps of his grandfather, a veteran of World War II who'd commanded great respect from those around him. Brad worked hard and was accepted into the United States Naval Academy, where he trained to become an improvised-explosive-device (IED) ordnance officer. In 2011, during a deployment to Afghanistan, he stepped on an IED during a mission with Navy SEALs. He suffered significant wounds to his face and was left permanently blind. "I have essentially failed at my job," he remembers thinking. "My job was to protect these guys. I'm supposed to be the one who can find these IEDs. I've got the metal detector, I'm the one walking out in front of the patrol, and here I missed one."

Brad was transported to Walter Reed National Military Medical

Center in Maryland to recover. When his family came to visit, he was particularly anxious about reuniting with his little sister Elyse, eight years his junior. He had relished playing the role of the hero to her; from his perspective, this dynamic had been the defining feature of their relationship. When Elyse had watched movies like *Top Gun* and *The Hurt Locker*, which Brad felt glamorized the military experience, he never corrected her impression. "To her, I was a badass," he writes. "She saw me as a guy who could do amazing stuff like jump out of planes, SCUBA dive, and take apart bombs. I liked the idea that maybe she bragged about me to her friends. I liked the idea that in her mind, I was what I had always hoped to be. I liked the idea that she was proud of me."

Now Brad felt he had failed Elyse. "She's gonna come into the hospital room, and I'm not gonna be this hero version of myself, wearing the white uniform and the gold buttons and the medals on my chest. I'm gonna be laid up in a hospital room with stitches all over myself and tubes coming out and I can't even get up to go to the bathroom by myself," Brad said.

But to Elyse, what actually defined their relationship were the everyday things that bond siblings—laughing over Brad's cheesy jokes, quoting *Saturday Night Live* sketches and Will Ferrell movies, and talking about their latest musical obsessions or travel experiences. That version of Brad was still fully intact, and Elyse reacted to his new state with only love and tenderness. This was a moment of revelation for Brad. "You know, it was kind of paradigm changing for me, realizing that this brother-sister relationship wasn't exactly what I thought it was," he said. Before his injury, he had never questioned *why* he'd felt that impressing Elyse was a critical part of their relationship. She had never once suggested that anything hung on his profession, nor that she'd even taken special pride in his accomplishments. Brad had absorbed these messages from other places, perhaps initially from how people responded to his grandfather, and then through his tenure in the Navy. "I realized that this hero thing was never actually part of *her* narrative," Brad said.

Empowered by this realization, Brad was able to be more forthcoming with Elyse and the rest of his family about his vulnerabilities, something he had long been loath to do. This shift in mindset was especially important during his recovery from the explosion, when it was essential that he be open about his emotional and physical needs. He remembers one afternoon when he and his guide dog got terribly lost walking around Baltimore. His instinct was to shield his loved ones from his struggles. But rather than give in to that impulse, he picked up his phone and called Elyse, who helped him find his way home.

If we can be intentional about seeing change as a moment to reexamine our beliefs, we might discover that they are not sacred, immutable truths. It can be tempting to think that we've arrived at each of our convictions through a process of thoughtful reflection and deliberate reasoning. Although this may be true for some of them, many others likely rest on flimsier ground—particularly those ideas we absorbed as young children, which can be bound up with our desire for love and belonging. We learned these ways of thinking and being when we were vulnerable and seeking safety, and when our brains weren't fully developed. But regardless of when we first formed our beliefs, we likely reached many of them via mental shortcuts—through intuition or through messages we absorbed, often subconsciously, from loved ones or from societal norms. We may also have been affected by the emotional state we happened to be in when processing the incoming information, or by who the messenger was. Or, like Ingrid, we may have overinterpreted or misunderstood the meaning behind what we were told. It's interesting to consider how, if our lives had unfolded in a slightly different way, we might have ended up with a drastically different worldview.

.

A few months after Ingrid's revelation about her family history, she opened up her laptop, eager to write. Her memories had more or less returned by this point, and her novel, the one she had started in her freshman writing class, was taking shape. It was inspired by her own life and featured a young girl named Chula, who grew up amid the kidnappings, car bombings, and assassination attempts of 1990s Bogotá. Ingrid was a third of the way through the manuscript, and she was hopeful that it could get published. But as she wrote each day, she began to wonder: Why was she cloaking her own story within the protective wrapper of fiction?

Ingrid searched through her laptop and found an old file containing five pages of the memoir she'd begun drafting in that class all those years ago. She started up again, furiously writing page after page of her memoir in parallel with her novel. When she called her mom to tell her about this new project, Sojaila implored Ingrid not to make their stories public, since it might expose Ingrid to ridicule or backlash. But Ingrid insisted—she was willing to take that risk. She dug into the colonial history of Colombia and the oppression that Indigenous people had endured. She researched curandero lore and read anthropology books about the rituals her family had practiced. She interviewed her relatives about her grandfather and returned to her family's village to speak with some of the people he had helped.

When Ingrid's novel, *Fruit of the Drunken Tree*, was finally published in 2018, she was elated. Everything she had dreamed of for herself as a writer was coming true. But the warm reception she received on her book tour only made her more impatient to tell the real version, the nonfiction version. She worked on her memoir whenever she could, the words spilling out of her on plane rides, in hotel rooms, and before and after live events. "I lived in a state of wonder, constantly overwhelmed with the richness of all my family stories, finally returned, learned anew," she would later write.

Ingrid's memoir, *The Man Who Could Move Clouds*, was published in 2022. It honors her cultural history and tells stories that her family has passed down over generations. It was chosen as a finalist for both the National Book Award and the Pulitzer Prize. Ingrid couldn't believe it—here, at last, her split identity had been made whole. "My amnesia allowed me to see that the shame I was carrying was just a block in my identity, a block I could take out—kind of like Jenga—and decide I didn't need," she said. "I can say, 'Ohh, I actually don't need that part of the story,' or 'That part isn't necessary.' Or 'Maybe it had a function at some point in my life, and it just really doesn't anymore.'" When Ingrid called her mom to celebrate the book's success with her, Sojaila responded cheekily, "Well, *obviously*. I mean, the stories are just so good."

⋅

In thinking about what we bring with us from childhood into adulthood, the therapist Abby Birk, inspired by the work of Dr. Emily Nagoski, uses a garden metaphor. Birk, whose therapy practice focuses on how our family origins shape us, writes the following:

> Each person is born with a garden; some plants are already planted in this garden at birth—without your say so—things like a sensitive nervous system, a predisposition for anxiety, depression, addiction or even a good memory, natural resilience, and other strengths. There are some seeds that have been planted generations before you and there will be some species of weeds that everyone inherits in the garden they are born with. As you mature, you begin to choose how to tend and manage this garden, what weeds you pull, and what plants you want to start growing instead.

An important component of this garden is our beliefs. As Birk explains, we can be intentional as adults about how we manage our gardens. When a change happens, it can be an opportunity to plant something new or to pull a few weeds.

When reexamining your beliefs, it is helpful to cultivate what is known as *metacognitive awareness*, which is when you think *about* your thinking. By reflecting on and turning a critical eye toward how exactly you've arrived at a belief, you might detect problems in your thought process. To aid with this, the author and psychologist Adam Grant, inspired by the work of the economist Arnaldo Camuffo, suggests adopting the mindset of a scientist. This means staying curious, embracing humility, questioning your assumptions, and treating your beliefs as hypotheses that should be tested. Thinking like a scientist involves actively seeking out data, even if they contradict your own views, and being careful not to tie your identity to any given viewpoint. As part of this shift in mindset, you can ask yourself the following questions: How did I get from point A to point B in my thinking? Based on what existing beliefs did I form this new one? Would this belief hold up against the scrutiny of the people I trust? In theory, what evidence *would* persuade me to change my mind? You can also engage in a thought experiment to test out the fragility of your ideas: Imagine that you were born in a different time period or place, or into a different culture or family—would you still have the same beliefs that you carry now?

In the years since her bout of amnesia, Ingrid has revisited other judgments about herself that were rooted in childhood. "I am aware of the power I have in editing my own stories, in updating them," she said. "And I feel the power to question who gave me the idea. How and why did I internalize a particular idea in the first place?" Most recently, she has been asking these questions in regard to her struggles with anxiety. Growing up, she thought it was a sign of weakness to express fear or show emotions. In the volatile environment of Bogotá, she absorbed the message to just "suck it up" and move forward. When bombs would blow out the windows of people's homes, for example, her neighbors often viewed it as nothing more than an inconvenience. And so, when Ingrid had panic attacks, she developed an internal narrative that she was weak. Now she is trying to construct a different narrative: perhaps her ability to endure painful panic episodes and to come out the other side intact is a testament to her mental fortitude.

Ingrid still relishes the lightness she felt when her memories were first erased, and she occasionally tries to practice "having amnesia." "I might be walking outside or in my home. I look and witness what is around me, trying to let the context of what I know of my surroundings fall away," she said. "If I didn't know what a highway was, how strange would it be to witness those metal containers go at great speeds, people staring forward like nothing strange is happening? It's a practice of defamiliarizing myself with my surroundings. It allows me to see things in new ways."

For weeks after her bike crash, Ingrid did not tell her family in Colombia that she'd been in an accident. But when she finally admitted to them what had happened, they were actually excited. It was common knowledge in the family that Sojaila, too, had experienced a bout of amnesia as a child, after falling down a well and hitting her head. This incident had unlocked her curandera powers. Maybe, the family thought, the bike accident would unlock the same abilities within Ingrid.

Ingrid never developed those abilities (her family likes to joke that she "did amnesia wrong"), nor does she fully believe in her family's healing powers. But from Ingrid's perspective, the amnesia still gave her a powerful gift. "Both of our accidents led to a new way of seeing things. I used to think that my identity had to contain whatever narratives were given to me—that I had limited control over it. But now I feel that how you view your family's history is a choice you can make."

6

A City of Refuge

aryann Gray couldn't remember a time in her life when
she had felt so free. As she rolled fresh paint onto the
blemished walls of the bedroom she was moving into,
she sang along to her favorite Joni Mitchell record. The roller glided
effortlessly. With each row of paint, the wall looked increasingly
smooth and pristine. Was it necessary to let the first coat dry fully
before rolling on the next layer? She wasn't sure, but that was the fun
of it—she could be spontaneous and just figure it out. So on she
went, painting and singing as the first of her moving boxes sat in the
corner of the room, ready to be unpacked.

It was June 15, 1977, and Maryann was twenty-two years old. She'd
recently dropped out of a clinical psychology master's program in
Oxford, Ohio, to join a commune called Southern Rainbow in a dilapidated mansion in Cincinnati. Earlier that day, she had completed
the first of the back-and-forth trips she'd need to make from Oxford

to Cincinnati, cramming as many of her belongings as she could into her car for the thirty-mile drive. As soon as she finished moving in, she planned on finding a minimum-wage job.

Maryann's decision to quit the master's program had come as a shock to her parents; they valued the status and security that came with an advanced degree. Maryann had never defied their wishes like this before. Born and raised in the affluent suburb of Scarsdale, New York, she was a self-described "goody-goody," with all the perfectionist tendencies the label implied. She attended college at Duke University and then enrolled in the clinical psychology program at her mother's insistence. Two years in, though, Maryann realized she was miserable. She was training to be a therapist, but felt emotionally immature herself. Given her inexperience in romantic relationships and her difficulties navigating her own family's interpersonal conflicts, what advice could she possibly offer her struggling patients? And then there was a more personal concern: Was a career as a therapist what Maryann really wanted? Or was this just another instance of her trying to color within the lines, anxious to satisfy her parents' expectations?

The more Maryann reflected on it, the more convinced she became that the story she was living out wasn't one she had chosen for herself. "I wanted to live a more authentic life. Even though I didn't know what my heart wanted yet, I wanted to find it and live that way," she said. Quitting her graduate program and moving into Southern Rainbow, alongside eight other twenty-somethings who espoused ideals of peace and togetherness, seemed like a great first step in her self-exploration.

Maryann laid down her paint roller and stepped back to survey her work. Her new bedroom was now a warm and inviting yellow, a vibrant, fresh color for a vibrant, fresh start—a nice contrast to her dull-brown apartment back in Oxford. By all measures, the day had been a resounding success. Tomorrow, Maryann would load more of her belongings into her car and make another trip, maybe two, and that would be that. She cleaned up her paint supplies, collected her things, and hopped into her car for the drive back to Oxford.

She was just a few miles from her old apartment, cruising by some ranch houses, when a young boy with blond hair materialized on the road, darting out from behind a row of mailboxes. Maryann started to swerve, but at forty-five miles per hour there was little time to move out of the way. She heard a sickening thud.

She pulled over to a side street and stepped out of her car. A crowd had gathered around the boy, who'd been tossed through the air. There was blood on the road. Maryann ran behind a bush on the front lawn of a nearby house, hiding like a child, but screaming all the while. A woman in a housedress raced out of her front door crying "Brian! Brian!" But as she ran toward the boy, her knees gave out. Two other women eased her onto the stoop of her home and held her steady, desperate to shield her from what had happened to her son. Help finally arrived and Brian was taken to the hospital. Only then did Maryann emerge from behind the bush and return to the road. Some police officers were talking to a small group of people. When Maryann spotted them, she raised her hand and exclaimed, "I did it, I did it!"

Maryann was asked to sit in the back seat of a patrol car. Two officers then asked her questions about what had occurred and requested that she issue a formal statement. She began praying for Brian. *Dear God*, she started. *Please let him be okay. He's just a kid. I'll do whatever you want.*

Another officer soon approached the patrol car with some news: Brian had died. A kindly neighbor came to the car to offer Maryann a cup of water and a cold, damp towel. She then invited Maryann to sit with her in her kitchen, while they waited for the sheriff's office to complete their evaluation. Some time later, the lead officer came to speak with Maryann. The police had completed their review, which involved interviewing those who had witnessed the accident. There was no indication that Maryann had done anything wrong. She was free to go home, but the officer implored her to "never do anything like this ever again." Even in her shock and grief, Maryann was furious. *Never do this again?* Did he really think she'd planned this?

Maryann was in no state to drive. She phoned one of her old professors from the clinical psychology program, who came with his pregnant wife to pick her up. On the ride home, Maryann wept as she recounted the details of what had happened. She then felt guilty that the professor's wife would now worry that *her* future child might get hit by a car one day. Maryann also thought about her own parents, whom she had yet to call. They might be destroyed emotionally—and, if Brian's family sued, financially too. It was easier for Maryann to obsess over concerns like these than to confront the enormity of what had happened.

Later that evening, Maryann summoned the courage to phone her parents. "It was an accident, Mommy," she cried out, referring to her mom in a way she hadn't since childhood. "Of course it was," her mom responded. Despite this assurance, Maryann was haunted by fear and remorse. In the weeks that followed, she refused to leave her packed-up apartment in Oxford. She was afraid to go outside, in case she unintentionally hurt another person. Driving was out of the question. She didn't want to talk to anyone, out of concern for what they might think of her. Whenever she saw a neighbor walk by her window, she ducked out of sight.

In her self-imposed isolation, Maryann felt incapable of carrying out basic tasks. The simple act of brushing her teeth was now an overwhelming experience, tears streaming down her face as she imagined Brian's child-sized toothbrush. She tried to distract herself with chores like washing dishes or wiping down countertops, but she inevitably got caught up in the intrusive images that played on a loop in her mind: Brian cartwheeling in the air, his mother crying, blood on the road. When she came to, she would notice that she'd been wiping and re-wiping the same spot on the counter.

Eventually, Maryann decided to attempt a small task with clear step-by-step instructions. She began baking cookies using a recipe she'd first learned in a home-economics class in middle school. "I creamed butter and sugar until my arms ached, and then I napped. I baked. I slept. I baked. I slept," she said. She wanted to give these cookies to the people who had helped her on the day of the accident, but she had no way to deliver them because she couldn't bring herself to leave her apartment. She baked batch after batch after batch, until the ingredients ran out. Then she threw the cookies away.

•

Maryann knew, in the rational part of her mind, that she wasn't morally responsible for Brian's death. She hadn't been drinking, she hadn't been speeding, and she hadn't been careless. The people Maryann spoke to about the accident—the police officers, the witnesses, her professor and his wife, her parents—all assured her that it was just that: an accident. But this notion was intolerable to Maryann. For so much of her life, she had tried to be good and do good. And yet she'd caused this terrible thing to happen. Did this mean that, despite her best efforts, she might somehow cause *another* terrible thing to happen? It was troubling to think that the universe could be so callous.

Perhaps, Maryann thought, she *did* deserve to suffer somehow. Maybe she was being punished for violating her parents' wishes—for having been on that road at all, when really she belonged back in Oxford, completing her master's degree. Or maybe it was something worse. An idea began to take shape for Maryann: maybe she had brought about this tragedy because she was a bad person who unleashed bad things into the world.

She was drawn to this logic partly because of a book she'd read called *Handbook to Higher Consciousness* by Ken Keyes Jr. In Maryann's reading of the book, people are the creators of their own realities: happy people live in a happy world, sad people live in a sad world, loving people live in a loving world. It was this message that had inspired Maryann to defy her parents' wishes in the first place— to drop out of school and finally be the author of her own narrative.

If everybody manifested their realities, and Maryann's actions had created a dangerous reality, she reasoned that it could mean only one thing: somewhere deep in the core of her being, *she* must be danger- ous, too, in ways that were only now being revealed. "I felt my dark side was so dark and so powerful that it had lured Brian into the road," she said. She decided that she would need to live in a state of vigilance to protect others from herself.

Everywhere she looked, Maryann now saw the potential for peril. She placed potted plants on the sides of her porch, under the guise of decoration, to indicate to visitors that the porch had a sudden drop- off. She kept her sink free of any knives. And even though she had always loved children, she no longer allowed herself to be around them, for fear she might somehow harm them.

Over the next few years, Maryann tried to put her life back to- gether, creating, if not a fresh start, then at least a new set of life cir- cumstances. She moved to California, where she completed graduate work in social psychology, became a research scientist at the RAND Corporation, and then joined the administration at the University of Southern California. She settled into an orderly life in which she fo- cused on her career. She also started seeing a therapist. With some practice, she regained the courage to drive, albeit slowly when on the highway. But on the inside she knew that she could never grow inat- tentive. *If my dark side escapes the clutches of my consciousness again, who knows what might happen?* she wondered. She would hear Brian's voice in her ear, saying, "Don't get too happy. Remember what happened the last time you felt happy." She heard the voice so frequently that she gave it a name: Inner Brian.

Inner Brian was a constant companion. He spoke to Maryann all through the day and late into the night, sometimes offering nothing more than a hello, and at other times delivering messages that were cruel and demanding. He belittled her whenever she made a mistake. He reminded her that children would never be safe around her. He scolded her whenever she'd gone a few hours without having thought about the real Brian. "You almost forgot about me," Inner Brian would say. "If you ever forget about me, you'll be sorry."

The idea that the world is fundamentally fair is captured by the *just-world hypothesis*, a concept introduced by the psychologist Melvin Lerner in the 1960s. In a just world, people get what they deserve. In 1975, the psychologists Zick Rubin and Letitia Anne Peplau developed the Just World Scale by administering a twenty-question survey that asked participants to rate how much they agreed with statements like "It is rare for an innocent man to be wrongly sent to jail," "When parents punish their children, it is almost always for good reasons," and "In almost any business or profession, people who do their job well rise to the top." The results showed that people run the gamut in how much they believe in a just world.

As a child, Maryann developed a strong belief in a just world in large part due to her parents' influence. They told her that if she was good, which for them meant following the rules, studying hard, and pursuing a reputable career, then good things would happen in her life. When she ran into difficulties, like feeling lonely and awkward on the playground, her mother insisted that it was simply a matter of time before everything turned her way. "I took refuge in my mother's narrative," Maryann said. "My fantasy, which she nurtured, was that I was an ugly duckling who would emerge one day as a swan. Instead of being weird-looking and insecure, I would be self-assured and popular."

When Maryann eventually made the decision to leave graduate school and break with her parents' values, she still managed to rationalize her choice within a just-world framework: she *was* being good, albeit in a way that was now defined differently. "*Handbook to Higher Consciousness* was saying, 'Oh, the hell with grades and career, focus on your spiritual well-being and your happiness,'" Maryann said. "I could cultivate love inside myself and then get that back from the universe."

The idea of a just world is communicated to many of us early and often. It is reflected in idioms like "You reap what you sow," in the concept of karma, and in the moralities of many religions. There's an understanding, especially in Western culture, that we are the masters of our fates—that our success relies far more on our choices than it does on our luck. When everything is going well, we may be all the more inclined to believe this. It's satisfying to think that the good things in our lives are *our* doing. And of course, our inputs do matter, and in some contexts they matter a lot.

How strongly we each believe that we control our life outcomes depends on where our *locus of control* lies. This concept was developed by the psychologist Julian Rotter. If you have more of an *internal locus of control*, you think your life is governed primarily by your actions; if you have more of an *external locus of control*, you tend to attribute outcomes to external causes, chance, or fate. Studies show a correlation between having a strong internal locus of control and greater well-being.

But, when bad things happen, having a strong internal locus of control—a natural corollary to a belief in a just world—can lead to undue self-blame. For Maryann, it wasn't that the road was designed poorly, or that the placement of the mailboxes was hazardous, or that Brian maybe hadn't checked both ways before crossing the street. It was that *she* was dangerous.

Maryann's reaction may sound extreme, but it can be common to blame yourself for outcomes that were likely out of your hands. Take my friend Scott, a self-proclaimed "health nut" who was diagnosed with stage 4 bone cancer in his early thirties. Before his diagnosis, Scott had spent much of his adult life carefully tweaking his lifestyle to optimize his health. He slept nine hours each night, ate a plant-based diet, did high-intensity training regularly, and carried around chia seeds to sprinkle onto his meals. When he received his diagnosis, he immediately questioned whether he had followed the "correct" wellness plan. Had he not been healthy enough? Could he have prevented the cancer by following a different diet? He thought that because he had taken credit for the good stuff in his life—his admission to Harvard, for example, which he believed validated the choices he'd made up to the end of high school—he had to take responsibility for the bad stuff too. "Whether it's physically, nutritionally, spiritually," he said, "if I feel like I can move the needle positively, then it seems that maybe I somehow moved the needle negatively."

I mentioned to Scott, after he'd finished a successful treatment for his cancer, that perhaps there was no way he could have avoided getting sick, that maybe it didn't have anything to do with his choices. Scott said that, on a rational level, he agreed, but the emotional part of his brain resisted this message. He wanted to believe his past choices had led to his cancer, because then he could also believe he had control over his future—like whether he could prevent a relapse. Though it was uncomfortable to blame himself for his cancer, it was better than feeling like he had limited say over how the rest of his life turned out.

Sometimes, to feel like a situation is more just, we tell ourselves certain stories. Perhaps we search for a lesson in our misfortune, or some other silver lining: "Was my old self that great?" Scott recalled wondering. "Perhaps the cancer suggests that what I needed was a good ass kicking in some way." Or maybe we believe that a greater force—karma, fate, God—is ultimately balancing the scales, even if we can't understand how. Perhaps a twist in the road is, as my Hindu grandmother told me growing up, a form of divine punishment, a consequence of a poor choice in a previous life.

Maryann believed she had caused Brian's death because she had a dark, dangerous essence. Now it was incumbent upon her to atone for what she'd done to Brian, and to contain her essence so that it could not harm anyone else. As Inner Brian constantly reminded her, she had caused profound suffering, and therefore she, too, deserved to suffer. In the years following the accident, she entered dysfunctional relationships in which she allowed herself to be mistreated, and she denied herself meaningful friendships. When she eventually met her husband, Glen, she chose not to have children as another form of punishment. To enjoy life was a kindness she could not grant herself.

·

On July 16, 2003, Maryann was walking in her office building at USC when she found her coworkers huddled around a TV. Somebody had driven a car into the stalls of the Santa Monica Farmers Market. Witnesses were already using the word "massacre" to describe it. Sirens blared and helicopters circled the wreckage.

Maryann knew people who lived in the area and frequently visited the market. As the day passed, she anxiously called old friends and colleagues to make sure they hadn't been there. Phone call by phone call, she was reassured to hear that no one she knew had been harmed. But she was horrified to learn of the full impact of the crash: ten people had been killed, and more than sixty had been injured.

The driver was an eighty-six-year-old man named George Weller. His car had plowed through the market at more than forty miles per hour, which Weller said happened because he mistook his car's accelerator for the brake. Footage of the crash played across news channels. Maryann saw images of Weller emerging from his car in a daze, to furious screams of "Murderer!" Radio stations broadcast interviews with the bereaved and the injured. Meanwhile, details about those killed in the crash emerged; among them were a married couple, elderly shoppers, and young children.

At work the following day, Maryann struggled to concentrate. She couldn't help but draw parallels between the crash at the farmers market and her accident. Her mind kept drifting to Weller, the man whom many had already deemed evil. Quietly tucked between the excoriations of Weller were small details of his life: to those who knew him, he was a grandfather, a good neighbor, and a churchgoer. Little had been confirmed about what, exactly, had led to the crash, but many people had already made up their minds about Weller's intentions, with some even claiming that he had shown determination behind the wheel. Maryann's own experience, however, made her want to give Weller the benefit of the doubt. Was it too much to contemplate that the crash had been an accident?

The instinctive response that many in the public had toward Weller was something that the psychologist Melvin Lerner might have expected. One consequence of tightly holding on to the belief in a just world is not simply that we may blame ourselves when things go wrong for us; we also may blame others when things go wrong for *them*—whether they've been directly harmed themselves or, like Maryann and possibly Weller, have unintentionally caused harm. Lerner came to this realization in the 1960s, when he was struck by the strange behavior of health-care providers who were looking after mentally ill patients. Many of these providers, who were otherwise compassionate, seemed to hold these patients responsible for any suffering they experienced, speaking about them in demeaning and disparaging terms. This was likely a coping mechanism: it may have been easier to believe that the patients were to blame for their own pain than to accept the far more devastating reality that the universe had been randomly cruel to people who had done nothing to deserve it.

Lerner and his colleague Carolyn Simmons tested this hypothesis in a series of studies. In one notable 1966 study, participants watched as a person—the "victim"—was given electric shocks. (Unbeknownst to the participants, the victim was an actor and wasn't really being shocked.) When the participants were unable to intervene and stop the shocks, they were more likely to devalue and disparage the victim. Since this experiment, many studies have found a correlation between the belief in a just world and the blaming and disparagement of others, including poor people in developing countries, people with disabilities, people involved in accidents, patients with AIDS and cancer, and victims of rape. Rubin and Peplau, the developers of the Just World Scale, note that to "resent an innocent victim of circumstance seems an unusual reaction. But it is precisely the sort of reaction we would expect from people who tend to perceive victimization in terms of an underlying moral order." This instinct to have a lower opinion of those less fortunate, and a higher opinion of those more fortunate, exists even in very young children. In one study, kids as young as five years old tended to dislike people who were unlucky (for example, those whose soccer game got rained out) and to like people who were lucky (for example, those who found five dollars on the street).

According to Lerner, people who believe in a just world will sometimes go to irrational lengths to interpret evidence in a way that allows them to keep that belief alive. Not knowing why things have gone a certain way for others can fill us with such gut-level discomfort that our minds search for a story to rationalize away any injustice. How else can we feel good about the world we live in? And how else can we reassure ourselves that we are not vulnerable to a similar fate?

Another reason we might blame others for their misfortune is that doing so can help us maintain some aspect of our own identity. This was the case for Christy Warren, a firefighter who routinely dealt with life-and-death situations that tested the limits of her control. Christy told me that she and several of her coworkers had developed a subconscious coping mechanism for when rescues weren't successful. They would search for reasons why the people they hadn't been able to save had somehow "deserved" their fate, when, in reality, they were likely just victims of bad luck. Christy might, say, blame a driver for having been in a dangerous part of town at night. This way of thinking helped her ward off an identity crisis. "We're rescuers—that's who we are," she said. "And if we don't rescue somebody, then we've done something wrong, and we're not rescuers anymore."

In Santa Monica, many were eager to villainize Weller in part because of what it would imply if he were not a villain: that at any moment we, too, might unintentionally inflict harm on others. The more Maryann thought it over, the more convinced she became that perhaps Weller needed some compassion, even if he hadn't been faultless. Maryann's accident had occurred when she was twenty-two; she'd had more than twenty years to process the darkest day of her life and to try to make amends. Weller had cut short ten lives. How long did he have left, at the age of eighty-six, to make amends for the awful tragedy he'd been responsible for?

·

The day after the crash at the farmers market—after repeatedly trying and failing to work—Maryann finally shut the door of her office, picked up a pen, and began to write. The tragedy, she wrote, was devastating, and her heart went out to those who'd lost loved ones. At the same time, she felt empathy for Weller, given her own experience. She had thought of Brian every day for the past twenty-five years, including on her wedding day and the day her dad died. And, in her soul, she apologized to Brian and his family every day too. She shared that she had decided against having children primarily because she feared she couldn't keep a child safe. She wrapped up her reflections by saying that she forgave Weller for losing control of his car at the farmers market.

Maryann set her pen down. As she read what she had written, she contemplated what she'd learned from reckoning with her own accident: good intentions weren't always enough; everyone carried within them the capacity to cause inadvertent harm. She felt a strong need to share this sentiment with others. Before she could talk herself out of it, she turned to her computer and visited NPR's submissions page. She typed out what she had written and clicked Enter.

Within an hour, her phone rang: *All Things Considered* wanted to air her piece. The next morning, Maryann was in a recording booth, reading aloud the words she'd drafted just a day prior. She then went home and nervously passed the time as she waited for the broadcast. When her voice finally came on the air, she sat glued to the radio, bracing herself for the backlash.

But the backlash never happened. Instead, Maryann received an outpouring of kindness, from people she knew and didn't know alike. They expressed sympathy for what she had been through, appreciation for her nuanced perspective, and admiration for her bravery.

The next day, the provost of USC called Maryann into his office. *Oh, no*, Maryann thought. *I'm really in trouble now.* She knew that many of her coworkers at the university—none of whom she had ever told about Brian—listened to NPR during their commutes. But rather than admonish her, the provost expressed his support. He was proud of Maryann. His wife was a clinical psychologist who wrote about post-traumatic stress, and she was interested in sharing her work with Maryann.

Maryann's eyes welled with tears. She had resigned herself to a life spent enduring the grief and guilt of her accident privately. "To take a risk and be vulnerable, to do something new and find out that it's received and appreciated in the spirit in which it's intended—it was very powerful for me," she said. "To tell your story to someone who's willing to be with you in that pain and not back away from it, it opened up all of this energy and hope that I had never experienced."

The overwhelmingly positive response to the NPR essay, which received more listener mail than any other segment that week, illuminated a previously inaccessible line of thinking for Maryann. When she had first heard about what happened at the farmers market, she instinctively felt compassion not just for the victims but for Weller too. And now all these strangers had heard *her* story and were extending that same compassion to her. If, as Maryann had announced to six million people across the country, she could extend forgiveness to the man responsible for the farmers market crash, couldn't she also forgive the twenty-two-year-old woman who had hit Brian?

One of the first people Maryann spoke to after the NPR broadcast was a good friend's older sister, who had killed a girl on a bicycle while driving. On the phone, the two compared their experiences and the devastation that had followed. The conversation marked the first time Maryann heard someone say out loud, "That happened to me, too." What had always seemed to her a solitary burden was, in fact, a shared one. Was it possible, Maryann wondered, that her story was more common than she'd thought?

She searched the internet, eager to connect with more people. She found websites for those who had been hit by a vehicle, but none for those who had been driving. There appeared to be no support groups for people like her. Eventually, she searched for "accidental killer." It was then that she came across a headshot of a rabbi and, beneath his photograph, a single sentence: "In Chapter 35 of Numbers, we read that G-d speaks to Moses and directs him to tell the people of Israel that when they cross the Jordan and enter into the land of Canaan, they are to establish six cities of refuge where a person who accidentally kills another person must run."

Maryann discovered that according to ancient Jewish law, any accidental "manslayer" was to flee to the nearest such city of refuge. Once within the walls of that city, if the manslayer was deemed innocent, they would be protected from any "blood avengers"—relatives of the victim seeking revenge. The accidental manslayer would then be welcomed into the fold of the community, able to live in peace and without fear of scorn or retaliation. The book of Deuteronomy describes a hypothetical scenario that warranted this type of refuge: "As when a man goes into the forest with his neighbor to chop wood and his hand swings the ax to cut down the tree, and the head slips from the handle and hits his neighbor so that he dies—he shall flee to one of these cities and live."

For Maryann to see herself reflected in these ancient words, and to have her plight looked upon with such mercy, was a refuge in itself. "If I had been exiled to a city of refuge, I might not have needed to exile from myself," Maryann said. "My biggest regret is that I lived such a constrained life for so many years. I like to think I could have lived a bigger life had I had more compassion for myself."

Maryann had become so concerned with not harming others that she'd fallen into an isolating self-focus—one she characterized as a form of "narcissistic suffering." "At some point, I realized it didn't matter whether or not I felt I deserved therapy," she said. "I needed to do it because the world needed me to be a functional person." She couldn't balance the scales by punishing herself indefinitely; no amount of suffering would ever make up for the death of a child. If anything, she was making the world worse by adding her own suffering to the mix.

If Maryann truly wanted to honor Brian's life, the way to do that was to actively look outside herself. Since there was no existing community for people like her, she decided to create one. She set up a bare-bones website that she called Accidental Impacts, on which she posted a synopsis of her story, a handful of resources for those struggling with PTSD, and an open invitation for people to send her an email. One by one, fellow seekers of refuge found their way to the site; soon enough, Maryann was fielding a steady stream of emails. The more she communicated with accidental killers like herself, offering whatever resources, condolences, and empathy she could, the more she came to understand how well prepared she was to support them.

As messages continued to appear in her inbox, Maryann decided to write a letter of her own, to Brian's mother. Though she had considered doing this many times before, she had never mustered up the courage. As Inner Brian always reminded her, his family had every reason to hate her. But Maryann mailed the letter anyway. "So many of my regrets," she said, "were about what I had *not* done as a result of fear. I didn't want this to be another."

A few weeks later, her work phone rang. It was Brian's older brother.

Maryann hadn't included her phone number in the letter, but he had managed to find it online. His mother, he explained to Maryann, had passed away, and he had opened the letter instead. He told Maryann about the depth of his family's grief following Brian's death. He also asked her about her recollection of the day of the accident. Maryann answered his questions and acknowledged his pain as best she could. She did not ask for forgiveness, and he did not offer it. It was obvious he was angry. But toward the end of the call, his tone shifted, and he asked Maryann about *her* life after Brian's death. When she explained that she hadn't had children because she was afraid she might hurt them, he expressed, gently, that he hadn't known it had been hard for her too. Sitting in her office afterward, Maryann waited for Inner Brian to scold her for reaching out to his family, but he was silent. "For once, he truly had nothing to say," she said.

By 2019, Maryann's Accidental Impacts site had connected people all over the world. She registered the organization as a nonprofit; its mission today is to offer resources and support for those who have unintentionally killed or seriously injured others—a modern city of refuge in both spirit and practice. Three years later, in 2022, Accidental Impacts changed its name to the Hyacinth Fellowship. According to Greek mythology, the god Apollo and the mortal Hyacinthus were throwing around a discus when, by accident, Apollo's stray discus struck Hyacinthus in the head. Apollo held him in his arms as he died, and in his grief he raised a flower—what we now call a hyacinth—from his dear friend's blood. The flower was a symbol of remembrance, something beautiful by which Apollo could pay homage to the life he had accidentally taken.

When grappling with a difficult, unwanted change, it can be natural to try to make sense of what's happened within the framework of a just world. But there are some changes that occur for no meaningful reason and offer no lessons—they're just things that happen. And yet in these situations it can still feel satisfying to blame ourselves. Self-blame can be comforting, giving us the false sense that we are in control and are righting some wrong. But it can also take us down a path along which, like Maryann, we become consumed by shame. Because we feel irredeemable, we are unable to take constructive steps forward.

Research shows that one way to help prevent this response is to cultivate more self-compassion, using an approach developed by the psychologist Kristin Neff. According to Neff, self-compassion involves recognizing your suffering, mindfully engaging with your emotions, and understanding that the pain you're feeling is part of a shared human experience. This last element is particularly important: if you can contextualize an awful event in your life as something that can happen to other people, too, you're more likely to depersonalize it and shift toward a more external locus of control—to interpret it as something that's happened *to* you, as opposed to something that's happened *because of* you.

In one study on self-compassion, participants were asked to reflect on an event in their lives that made them feel shame. Some of these participants then completed a self-compassion writing exercise in which they were instructed to write to themselves with kindness and concern, to try to describe their feelings objectively, and to brainstorm the varied ways in which other people might have endured something similar. Those who completed this exercise experienced a significant reduction in their shame. By contrast, participants who were instructed to simply write expressively about whatever had triggered their shame—to "let it all out"—did not experience a decrease in shame. Other studies have further demonstrated that engaging in self-compassion exercises of this kind can lessen our shame and even reduce how often we form irrational beliefs.

Another powerful way to boost your self-compassion is, paradoxically, to reorient your focus outward and help others, just as Maryann did by forming the Hyacinth Fellowship. Research shows that people regularly underestimate the positive impact they're able to have on others; shame-prone people are especially likely to think that they can't be of value. This kind of thinking gives rise to a vicious cycle. If you believe that you have nothing to offer, you're more likely to withdraw from the world. If you withdraw from the world, you contribute less to it, and this only confirms your initial suspicion that you aren't valuable and are therefore unworthy of self-compassion. One way to break this cycle is to take that first step and engage with others. When you see your impact up close—whether it's helping a friend move into their new apartment, cheering up a stranger who is looking glum, or counseling a coworker on how to navigate a tough project—it can begin to dispel your shame. As Dr. Vivek Murthy, the former U.S. surgeon general, told me, "What service does is it allows us to connect to somebody else in an environment where we are truly helping them in a way that's immediate. But we also reaffirm to *ourselves* that we have value to bring to the world."

I first met Maryann in the early winter of 2022. I was taken by her unflinching honesty and self-awareness. We developed a fast friendship, bonding over being social scientists and how that background had informed our perspectives on the world. She shared with me a trove of her personal writing since Brian's death, and one day as I sat reading, I learned that shortly after creating her nonprofit, she searched online for the road that had changed her life's trajectory. She discovered that the spot where the crash had happened was part of a fourteen-mile stretch of Route 27 near Oxford, Ohio, which had earned itself the moniker "Highway to Heaven," due to the number of fatal accidents that had occurred there. In 2000, *Reader's Digest* listed the Highway to Heaven as one of the nation's most dangerous roads.

Maryann could have spent her years blaming the highway, rather than herself, for Brian's death. But, as she explained to me, things were not that straightforward. "This isn't about getting rid of pain, or saying 'I'm a wonderful person' in the mirror every day," she said. "I didn't intend to run over an eight-year-old boy—but what would it say about me if I didn't feel guilty?" She also told me that she no longer ascribed inherent meaning to all the events in her life; her belief in a just world had weakened over time. "Why was I the one who hit and killed Brian? It's just not that interesting of a question anymore," she said. "The much better question is, what am I going to do about it?"

In the same way a change can lead us to revisit our relationships and our beliefs about our families, it can also give us an opportunity to reexamine our foundational ideas about how the world works. Maryann did just that when she loosened her grip on her belief in a just world. This new orientation allowed her to build a life in which she was able to help other people—something that had once felt impossible. Her work with the nonprofit, she said, was probably the most meaningful element of her life, and she believed that it had also made her a better person. "I'm more authentic and direct in my interactions with people," she said. "I trust myself to be kinder and more helpful to those around me." At times, she was uneasy about having a spotlight on her. "But this work is important, and it means something to people," she said. "And so, damn it, I'm going to do it—uncomfortable or not." As she looked back on the nearly seventy years of her life, she noted that she had not had children, had not written a bestseller, and had not invented anything. "But I have done this," she said, referring to her work with the Hyacinth Fellowship, "and I hope it will live beyond me."

During our final conversation, Maryann disclosed that she had been battling a health issue and would require a bone-marrow transplant. She died on April 1, 2023, due to complications from the procedure. More than a hundred people showed up for her memorial to share stories—about her work ethic, her wit, the mean right hook she swung in her boxing classes, and how the Hyacinth Fellowship had supported so many. As we wrapped up our last chat, Maryann told me, "I feel like I've done some good in this world, which—fair or not fair—I hadn't felt before. I can look back now and say, 'I've left a little bit of a mark.'"

7

The Missing Piece

I met Jimmy on a warm summer evening in 2014 in Washington, D.C. We shared mutual friends and had both been invited to a small dinner at a Chinese restaurant. When Jimmy walked in and came over to introduce himself, I was struck by his bright, sweet smile and his athletic build. His thick black hair, swept to the side on his forehead, resembled that of an Asian pop star. I felt a little jolt of excitement when he chose the seat next to mine. As we ate stir-fried noodles and garlic string beans, Jimmy shared funny, self-deprecating stories. He was a conscientious conversationalist—shifting the discussion to focus on others, posing thoughtful questions, and pulling in those we hadn't heard much from. As the dinner progressed, I found myself sneaking quick glances at him right after I told a story or made a joke, to see if he'd liked it.

We spent more time together in the following weeks, and I was charmed by Jimmy's enthusiasm for life and its everyday details. The night before playing in a squash tournament, he struggled to fall asleep because he was just too excited about competing. When he took bites of his favorite foods, he'd say, "You know, we didn't have to evolve to find food *this* tasty. I'd have eaten it anyway." One evening, as we walked to a restaurant together, Jimmy suddenly stopped in his tracks and proclaimed, "Man, isn't consciousness *so great*, Maya?!" His love of life was infectious. I remember thinking how lovely it would be if I could do this life thing alongside him.

But I wasn't sure whether he liked me back, and my nerves were beginning to show. One afternoon, Jimmy invited me to lunch at a local tea shop. As we sat in the shop's rickety wooden chairs, we shared stories about being raised by Asian immigrant parents, how we'd both played the violin growing up (he quite reluctantly), and our common interest in neuroscience. We had an obvious chemistry, moving with ease between serious and lighthearted topics. At one point during the meal, I became so giddy that I forgot to check if the lid of my teapot was properly secured. When I went to pour tea into my cup, it spilled all over the table, sabotaging my plate of food and just barely missing Jimmy's. I was so embarrassed, but I still left the tea shop beaming. Later that night, I wrote in my journal, "Lunch today was delightful. In every sense. The conversation with Jimmy is just effortless and engaging and so sweet and cozy and awesome. Oh boy. I feel like a Taylor Swift song right now. All of them, combined!"

After six weeks of hanging out as friends, I decided to make Jimmy a personalized crossword puzzle that I hoped would make my feelings clear and encourage him to share if he had any in return. I spent hours coming up with the puzzle. The clue for 9 Across was: "This is the kind of love our Asian parents have for us." (One word, eleven letters.) The answer: *conditional*. Another clue roasted Jimmy for slacking off during his summer job: "This is the one document Jimmy submitted during his legal internship." (Two words, seventeen letters.) The answer: *resignation letter*. I'd also created a bonus clue, written on a separate sticky note. My plan was to make a game-time decision about whether it felt right to present this particular clue to Jimmy.

When I mustered up the courage to share the puzzle with him, he began solving the clues one by one, tapping into the rich set of memories and inside jokes we shared. Once he completed it, I reached over and handed him the bonus clue: "This is what Jimmy should've given Maya, but hasn't yet." (Two words, five letters.) The answer: *A kiss!* I looked up from the sticky note and saw that Jimmy was blushing. He gave me a knowing smile, and then, rather than seize upon what could've been a romantic moment, delivered a twenty-minute monologue about why he'd been too sheepish to tell me that he liked me. He even mentioned that he had *almost* kissed me during one of our previous hangouts. "Jimmy! For goodness' sake!" I exclaimed. He finally leaned in.

Our relationship felt serious from the get-go. We immediately developed a closeness that neither of us had felt with someone else before. But there was one subject that we had yet to cover: children. In several of our conversations, Jimmy had offhandedly mentioned that he was eager to share with his future kids the things he'd found enchanting in his own childhood—like the movie *Toy Story* or Roald Dahl's

Matilda. As taken as I was by these lovely images, every time the topic of parenthood came up, my body tightened. My mind would race, and I'd redirect the conversation as quickly as I could.

•

Growing up, I was enamored with the idea of motherhood. One afternoon, I watched an episode of *The Oprah Winfrey Show* that featured a woman named Kathryn, who was just months away from having her ninth child. I sat rapt on the couch in our family room as Kathryn went through her daily routine with all these cute little humans to care for. I was the youngest of four kids, and I relished the coziness and bustle of being part of a big family. As my two brothers and my sister each left the house for college, I felt a deep sadness. When it was time for me to move out of the room I'd shared with my sister and into the now empty bedroom of one of my brothers, I took out my colored markers and created a sign for the door. Instead of the typical "KEEP OUT!" my sign read "MAYA'S ROOM. PLEASE ENTER!"

In one scene of the *Oprah* episode, Kathryn squeezes in a quick workout while her toddler lies on the ground next to her, trying to imitate her crunches. I called my mom, who was at work at the time, and gushed to her about what I'd seen: the abundance of kids, the endless affection, the baby crunches! "I think I might want a big family for myself one day?" I told my mom, testing how the words sounded coming out of my mouth.

She chuckled. At the age of twenty-one, my mom had been introduced to my dad through an arranged meeting in Chennai, India. They had a formal marriage ceremony twenty days later. Then she quit her job as a fourth-grade teacher and joined my dad on a one-way flight to the United States, where they lived in a small dorm room on Harvard's campus while he finished his postdoctoral fellowship in physics.

My mom found her life in the States lonely. She'd grown up in a large family—with fifty-one first cousins—in India, where spontaneous visits from relatives and friends were standard. With thousands of miles now separating her from her homeland, she decided that she would try to re-create that warmth by having a large family of her own. As she and my dad raised the four of us, she didn't get a solid night's sleep for years and barely had time for herself. But despite the sacrifices and stress, she nevertheless relished her role as a mother. "It will be a ton of work, Maya," she told me that day. "But you can certainly have a big family, too."

I remember thinking that any amount of work would be worth it. For one, this imagined future with my children was a mental refuge— a place my brain visited when I faced challenges in my life or felt troubled by the suffering in the world around me. Although I was generally a bubbly, upbeat kid, I internalized other people's pain easily and often ruminated over it. When I was in middle school, my friend Katie lost her mom to cancer; the image of Katie forcing a generous smile at the memorial service seared itself into my memory. When I traveled to India as a young child and saw kids my age starving and sick on the streets, I was haunted by this reality. When there were difficult conflicts at home, there'd be a persistent sinking feeling in my stomach.

But in the fantasy family I conjured up, we'd all be magically protected from distress and sorrow. We would be happy and healthy and hardly ever fight. My kids would fit in and never worry about looking or feeling different. They'd have carefree personalities and revel in the uncomplicated joys of childhood. They'd be comfortable opening up to me, and as their mom, I'd advise and protect them.

And then there was the fact that motherhood also seemed like the greatest marker of success for a woman—something the culture expected of me. As the author Sheila Heti writes in her novel *Motherhood*, "In a life in which there is no child, no one knows anything about your life's meaning. They might suspect it doesn't have one— no centre it is built around." At family gatherings, a similar message echoed in the conversations I overheard between my aunties. "Who did she marry? Oh, she's not married yet? But wait . . . doesn't she want to have kids?" Even though I was an ambitious child, with my heart set on becoming a concert violinist, I was far more interested in what people had achieved in their personal lives. *But does the Olympic gold medalist have kids? If she doesn't*, I thought, *she is missing out on what I've been told gives life its deepest meaning.*

Perhaps that was why, in the summer after my senior year of high school, when it was clear that my dream of becoming a violinist was over, I found myself revisiting my other big dream of one day becoming a mom. I'd felt the loss of the violin acutely and was eager to anchor myself to something that could still be a part of my future.

Older now, I knew, of course, that it would not be that perfect unit I'd fantasized about as a kid, but it would still be a source of so much happiness.

One evening that summer, though, I was flipping through the channels on TV when I came across a rerun of *The Matthew Shepard Story*. The movie told the true account of a twenty-one-year-old gay college student at the University of Wyoming who'd been brutally murdered by two men in 1998. I couldn't stay on the channel for long because I found it excruciating to watch Matthew's story play out. This was not an unusual reaction from me, but on this particular evening, my brain connected a new set of dots. Maybe because the topic of motherhood had been so prominent in my mind, I imagined, for just a moment, how it would feel to be the *parent* of a child who suffered greatly. The mere thought made me want to vomit.

I began to spiral. My imagination ran wild, conjuring up all the ways my future children might suffer. My kids could be victims of a hate crime, or be diagnosed with childhood cancer, or develop debilitating depression, or get into a car crash. No amount of love, wisdom, or devotion from me could shield them from life's indiscriminate cruelty. And it wasn't just the fear that they might endure pain—there was also the selfish fear that *I* might not be able to bear their pain. Witnessing them in anguish might just push me into depths of despair I couldn't climb out of.

The idea seized me so completely that I struggled to breathe. I tried to shake off this new anxiety, but it wouldn't leave me. *You can't know that*, I thought. *You can't guarantee that.* It felt jarring now to think that I'd ever imagined my future family as a refuge. That night,

I slept in fractured bouts, waking every half hour. I thrashed around in bed, as if, with enough exertion, I could break out of the straitjacket my mind had woven.

•

In the weeks that followed, as I moved into my dorm room and started my new life in college, I continued to be tormented by these thoughts. Now that I was viewing the world through the eyes of a prospective mother, every bad thing I heard or read about suddenly felt personal and threatening. I tried my best to talk myself out of this way of thinking—to gain a more balanced view of the emotional risks of parenthood—but I was insensitive to reason when it came to this specific topic.

I hated the person I was becoming as a result of my obsessive, all-consuming anxiety. Once a thoughtful, attentive listener to my friends, I now avoided their problems, excusing myself whenever a sad story was recounted. Once playful and quick to laugh, I now felt a seriousness creep into my personality. Once curious about the world, I now withdrew from it, avoiding entire sections of the newspaper and most movies. I hardly recognized myself.

Sometimes I'd entertain the possibility of not becoming a mom, and I'd feel a glorious reprieve from my anxiety. But this release would be short-lived, because I'd remember just how much of my life's meaning depended on achieving this dream of mine. And so, inevitably, I'd go back to wanting to become a parent. I also convinced myself—through some sort of self-sabotaging logic—that even if I did find ways to quell my fears and push these worries from my mind, it was morally irresponsible to ignore them. How was it okay for me to blithely enjoy my present when my children might suffer so greatly in the future?

In Salman Rushdie's *Knife*, a memoir about his near-fatal stabbing, he makes reference to Room 101 from George Orwell's novel *1984*. Room 101 is a torture chamber in which each person is subjected to the very thing they fear most. Rushdie discusses how the "worst thing in the world" is different for any given person; for *1984*'s protagonist, Winston Smith, it is being attacked by rats. For whatever reason, my Room 101 was occupied by a child of mine suffering.

On a windy and bleak autumn afternoon during my sophomore year, worn down by the scary images that played on repeat in my head, I called my dad. He taught physics at my university, and his office was just up the street from my dorm. My dad is one of the funniest people I know, but, like me, he is quite sensitive. The most pain I ever saw him experience was when one of his children was in distress.

He dropped what he was working on, and we met each other halfway. I could see that my current state—tears streaming down my face, cheeks red from worry—was causing him pain. As we walked, our shoes pressing against the damp leaves that had fallen to the ground, he made an unusual detour and guided us toward a nearby cemetery. The air was cold, and we pulled our coats tight against the wind. We entered the cemetery through an impressive stone archway and were met by rows and rows of headstones. I reflected on the fact that all these people had once led complicated lives just like ours. After we looped around several rows, my dad stopped for a moment and gestured at the graves around us. "No matter what suffering we endure, this will be our fate," he said. "So never let your fears grow too big."

It is not always comforting to feel small and transient in the universe, but in that moment I felt lighter. My dad was offering me a way to zoom out, to see my anxieties set against the backdrop of a much larger timescale. I saw that from a cosmic perspective, at least, the stakes weren't as high as I'd believed. All suffering, however awful, eventually comes to an end. It is finite. I nodded and took the first full breath I'd taken in some time.

•

By the time I met Jimmy about a decade later, I had a better handle on my anxiety. As I finished college and pursued a PhD and then a postdoctoral fellowship in cognitive science, I was more proactive about reining in my worries. My experience with my dad in the cemetery had not resolved my fear, but it had shown me that it was possible to dampen it through a slight shift in perspective. Eager to encourage other positive mental changes, I did sessions of cognitive behavioral therapy, which helps people both recognize and challenge negative patterns of thinking and behavior. One of the most valuable lessons I learned was that I could see my thoughts as simply that: thoughts. Just because I felt them deeply and viscerally didn't mean that they carried profound truth or predicted the future. This realization was empowering.

But although I was now able to be far more functional day to day, my worries about parenthood still lay beneath the surface. Being this particular way made me feel lonely. Many people know they don't want to have kids, but I seemed to fall into a different category: I desperately wanted kids but did not feel that I had the right emotional constitution for parenthood.

A month or so into my relationship with Jimmy, we took a trip to a cabin in Virginia with a bunch of his former law-school classmates. On the second day of the trip, we were gathered inside, passing the time before we had to make dinner. It was the beginning of fall, and it was chilly; a fire roared in the cabin. We were clustered in small groups, some standing with drinks, others slumped on big old sofas. I took a spot in front of the fireplace because I tend to run cold, and, because Jimmy does, too, it ended up being just the two of us standing in front of the fire. And that is when, seemingly out of nowhere, I found myself spilling everything to him about my fraught relationship with motherhood: how I wanted to be a mom more than anything, but how seeing my kids in pain would paralyze me. What kind of parent would I be in this state? What kind of partner? On balance, I told him, the pain I felt witnessing other people's suffering often exceeded the joy I felt in seeing their happiness. Oh, and I had one final thing to share, something even I had learned only recently. After some unusual swelling in my foot, a rheumatologist had run a battery of blood tests on me. The results showed that I had high levels of a rare set of antibodies that affect pregnancy. If I were to carry a baby, these antibodies could significantly impede fetal heart development in the baby in utero, causing congenital heart blockage and other cardiac abnormalities. And so, because of these antibodies, if I ever did summon the courage to one day become a parent, I would likely pursue adoption.

When I was finally done with my stream-of-consciousness monologue, I realized that all this information now hung uncomfortably in the space between us. *Oh my God*, I thought. *Jimmy has seen only the cheerful version of Maya, the one who teases him and laughs over a tea-soaked lunch. Now he knows my biggest fear. Is this relationship over?*

After taking a moment to collect his thoughts, Jimmy told me that he could empathize with how my anxieties had colored my thinking. Although he'd never experienced fears about fatherhood, he could certainly relate to worrying excessively about things that were out of his control, like his health and the health of his family. He also said that he could imagine just how tortured I'd felt—to want something so much and yet have so much apprehension about it. "If you're open to it, I do think this is something we could try to work through together," he said gently. "And, yes, of course I'd love to explore adopting a child with you. I really think you would be an amazing mom."

Over the next few years, we reached various milestones as a couple, like introducing our parents to one another and getting engaged. (This time it was Jimmy who created a crossword puzzle. The final clue asked if I'd marry him. The answer: one word, three letters.) We also made progress in managing my fears. Jimmy highlighted all the ways our children could experience *joy*, shifting my focus away from their potential suffering. He also helped me build my confidence about the kind of mom I would be to our kids, mentioning things like my emotional intelligence and affectionate nature. And he reminded me that I wasn't going to be on my own: they would be his kids, too, and I'd be able to lean on him when things got hard. Gradually, I started to feel less anxious. At times, I even felt a giddy excitement at the prospect of raising children with Jimmy. For the first time in more than a decade, I reclaimed some of my childhood exuberance about becoming a mom. I finally decided that it was worth taking the leap. Jimmy and I would try to become parents.

We began looking into our options, researching adoption and talking to friends about their experiences. On one spring afternoon, Jimmy and I called one of my brothers to catch up, and he told us that a friend of his had recently had a baby with the help of a gestational surrogate. After the call, Jimmy asked me if I'd ever be open to having a biological child together through surrogacy. (Doctors had told me that because the antibodies I have affect only the womb, it would be possible for Jimmy and me to create healthy embryos.) Jimmy said that as we'd fallen in love, he'd found himself thinking more and more about the baby we might have together. I admitted that I had, too, and was open to exploring that option.

In the years that followed, we got married, moved from D.C. to California, and took the first steps toward building a family. I did two rounds of egg retrievals, and we froze our embryos at a nearby clinic. We also signed up with a surrogacy agency. Eventually, the agency matched us with Haylee, a kind and gentle-hearted woman who lived in Arkansas with her husband and three kids. She was wonderfully empathetic and honest, and Jimmy and I felt a strong connection with her from the beginning. In early 2020, she flew to California for an embryo transfer.

On the morning of the procedure, we all sat in the crowded exam room together, holding our collective breath. The doctor showed Jimmy and me the clear straw that held our female embryo. If the procedure went smoothly, the doctor said, there would be a 65 percent chance of a pregnancy. After dimming the lights, the doctor, with the help of an ultrasound technician, began the transfer. As I stared at the ultrasound screen, an image unexpectedly popped into my head: a Chinese Indian baby with my textured, tightly spiraled hair, beaming at me with Jimmy's smile. She just looked so, so happy.

I began to cry. I squeezed Jimmy's hand, trying to channel my emotion into something other than audible sobs. After a few more moments, the doctor announced that the transfer had gone well.

Jimmy and I invited Haylee to come to lunch at my workplace's café. The sun shone brightly. I was overjoyed. I made all sorts of cheesy jokes on the drive over: "Jimmy, careful! You're driving with a baby on board now!" When we arrived at my office's lobby, I printed a guest pass for Haylee and then sneakily created a second badge— this one for Karina Shankar Li. I handed them over to Haylee, who chuckled and played along, attaching both name tags to her sweater. I had always loved names that begin with a K, and Jimmy and I agreed that Karina was a beautiful choice. Her nickname could be Kiri.

Ten days later, just as Jimmy was about to drop me off at the airport for a short work trip, Haylee texted us to say that she'd received the results of her blood test: she was officially pregnant. We called her and cheered together, ecstatic and relieved. In my frenzied state, I ended up missing my flight and had to call the Southwest Airlines customer-service line to book a later one. The agent seemed perplexed by my cheerful banter. I might have been the happiest customer who'd just missed a flight that she had ever spoken to.

A few days after that, on a call with the surrogacy-agency coordinator, I marveled at how seamless the experience had been so far. "Maya," the coordinator gently reminded me, "this process is allowed to be easy sometimes."

It was a simple, comforting thought; maybe we'd all gotten exactly what we wanted the first time around. I sniffled and then let out a sigh. "Okay, fine," I said. "But I didn't know it could be this beautiful."

•

As soon as the pregnancy was confirmed, Jimmy and I booked plane tickets to Arkansas so that we could join Haylee for the first fetal heartbeat ultrasound. As the date approached, though, we heard news that the first cases of COVID-19 had been reported in our area. To be safe, we canceled our trip and instead joined the appointment by video call. When Haylee picked up, the first thing we saw was a black-and-white ultrasound screen from the clinic room in Arkansas. There was a small spot on the screen that was flickering. The doctor told us it was our baby's healthy beating heart!

That night, I got into bed early and pulled up pictures from the ultrasound on my phone, studying each one closely. It was hard for my mind to grasp that this was all finally happening, thanks to Haylee. When Jimmy got home, he sat on my side of the bed, and we chatted about how excited we were. At one point, he pulled out his phone to quickly check the time and saw that we'd missed a call and a message from Haylee. The message read "Guys. Are you awake?"

My stomach dropped. Arkansas was two hours ahead of us, and it was already past nine on the West Coast. Haylee wouldn't be calling this late unless there was an emergency. We called her back. When she picked up the phone, she spoke in a slow whisper.

"I woke up bleeding," she said. "For the last hour, I've been bleeding and cramping."

We immediately called our clinic's emergency line. Our nurse reassured us over the phone that Haylee might simply have a blood clot, which would not be a cause for major concern. She advised Haylee to get a repeat ultrasound first thing in the morning.

We woke up to a text from Haylee saying that she was already at the doctor's office, waiting to be squeezed into the schedule. She sounded scared. We desperately wanted to give her a hug. It'd be at least an hour until we heard any news.

When my phone eventually rang, it was Jimmy, who was at work trying to facilitate a call between us, Haylee, and our surrogacy agency. I soon heard Haylee's voice come on the line.

"Is everyone there?" she asked.

Jimmy and I both said yes before she could finish the question.

"Awesome," she said flatly. I distinctly remember hoping that her "awesome" was not a nervous reflex but a sign of good news.

"There was no baby on the ultrasound," she said. "What was there yesterday isn't there today."

Jimmy rushed to get home, and on the drive back he started a three-way call with his parents and me. We began explaining to them what had happened, and, midway through, I began to weep. Jimmy, upon hearing me cry, which I rarely do, cried too.

After the miscarriage, we worked with our surrogacy agency to ensure that Haylee had access to psychological support and other resources. We assumed that she would not want to try for another pregnancy, given what she'd endured. We extended our deep gratitude for what she'd done for us. But, to our surprise, she told us that she was intent on trying again, going so far as to say that she was in this with us until the very end. Jimmy and I were moved beyond words.

In the months that followed, COVID-19 spread across the world, and we had to put our plans to try for another pregnancy on hold indefinitely. I'd always been fairly resilient in the face of setbacks, bouncing back with optimism, aided by an awareness of how much worse life could be. But the loss of the pregnancy had me reeling.

My struggles navigating this period were ultimately what led me to start my podcast, *A Slight Change of Plans*. Jimmy and I converted our bedroom closet into a makeshift studio, stuffing moving blankets and towels into its corners to create a better acoustic environment. My first round of guests had experienced a diverse range of changes that bore little resemblance to mine, but as I listened to their stories I felt a strong sense of connection. We were all in the thick of it, trying to make sense of and move through a new set of circumstances.

That spring, vaccines became widely available, and Haylee, Jimmy, and I began planning for a second embryo transfer. A year and a half had passed since we'd last seen Haylee, and when she got off the plane in California, we ran over to her and gave her giant bear hugs. We'd become close over the past year, texting daily and sharing photos of our lives. Haylee felt like family. During the holiday season, we exchanged presents. She sent us a handmade wood carving in the shape of the United States, with a red line that connected a heart in Arkansas to a heart in California.

The embryo transfer went smoothly; once again, there was a 65 percent chance of a successful pregnancy. Ten days later, Haylee sent us a screenshot of her blood test results, which showed a positive pregnancy. We were elated. The genetic testing had revealed that it was a female embryo, and we decided to give the baby the same name we'd originally chosen. I set up an email address for Karina and sent her a celebratory note that she could one day read. It began:

Fri, Aug 20, 2021, 12:32 PM
To: Karina, Haylee, Jimmy

Hi little Kiri!!
Yesterday was a very exciting day—Aunt Haylee, your
Dad, and I found out that you exist!

I signed off my note with a "Love, Mom." It gave me chills. I couldn't believe I was able to write that.

•

The following month, I'd just wrapped up a morning workout when I went to the kitchen sink to fill up my water bottle. I glanced down at my phone, which was sitting on the counter. Haylee had sent Jimmy and me a text.

"I just had a gush of blood . . . I'm on hold with the clinic," she wrote.

Haylee went in for an ultrasound, and Jimmy and I joined via video call. Jimmy tried to prepare me for the worst, but I clung to hope. The doctor conducting the ultrasound seemed tailor-made for the situation; he had a kindly Southern drawl and a calming presence. As he moved the ultrasound probe around, we received reassuring news fairly quickly. Haylee did in fact have a blood clot in the area, which meant there was another explanation for her bleeding. The doctor continued moving the probe and, after locating the fetus, told us that our baby's heartbeat was strong. Then he moved the probe around a bit more to make sure his examination had been thorough. We all saw something shocking when he did—there was another baby in there! Our embryo had split into identical twins.

I have a video recording on my phone of our response to this news: I'm shaking and squealing and laughing and putting my hand over my mouth as I process it all. "Well," Haylee said later that afternoon, with her typical deadpan delivery, "you better start picking out a second name."

Jimmy suggested we go on a walk to get some fresh air after our roller-coaster morning. We joked about how it might finally be time to move out of our small apartment. I shared how comforting it was to know that our twins would each have a built-in friend who could be there for them when life got hard. As soon as we returned home, I reinstalled the What to Expect app on my phone, which I had anxiously deleted that morning after receiving Haylee's initial message. Then I texted Haylee to see how she was feeling.

It was around four in the afternoon when I saw that Haylee was typing a reply. She started and stopped. Then started and stopped again. With each second that passed, my heart raced faster. I stared at the WhatsApp screen, as the "Haylee is typing" indicator flickered on and off. Finally, a text appeared: "I just passed something different than the clots that I've been passing. I emailed the clinic with a picture. But I want you to be aware that something happened. I just don't know what."

The next call we got was from our doctor at the clinic. "I'm so sorry, you guys," she said. "I can't believe this happened again." After an ultrasound confirmed the miscarriage, the doctor explained that it was likely due to a biological incompatibility between our surrogate and our embryo. "Given the testing we did," she told us, "this is likely not a result of a genetic issue with the embryo, but a systemic response in Haylee's immune system that might be rejecting your embryos."

I asked Jimmy if we could take another walk—our apartment was making me feel claustrophobic. It was a beautiful summer evening. The air was breezy and cool, and as we walked through the park, dogs ran around with their owners, playing fetch with tennis balls. I saw a young couple patiently teaching their kid how to ride a bike. Others walked with babies in their strollers.

•

That evening, back in our apartment, I crawled under the covers of our bed, feeling sad and overwhelmed. "Mayi," Jimmy said, using his pet name for me, "let's try something. Let's list five things we're each grateful for." I really didn't want to. The idea of expressing gratitude after a day like this felt jarring. I sat in silence for a moment and then looked up at Jimmy's reassuring face. He rattled off a few items on his gratitude list. I couldn't help but smile as I realized that I was looking at the person who would sit atop my list.

I was grateful, I began, for the strength of our relationship—how well we understood each other, and how our interactions were filled with so much laughter and warmth. I was grateful for my family and my best friends. For my coworkers, some of whom I'd worked with for more than a decade, who infused my work life with passion, humor, and optimism. My morning cups of steaming hot chai with freshly cut ginger, which had become a ritual for me over the past year—a way of grounding myself in something comfy when it felt like the world was spinning around me. The radiance of the California sun. The fulfillment of hosting *A Slight Change of Plans* and connecting with both my guests and my listeners. My health and ability to do Zoom workouts with my unflinchingly positive fitness trainer, Matt, with whom I loved to gossip about celebrities or the latest episode of *The Bachelor*. As my gratitude list flowed out of me, I realized something: I'd become so zeroed in on my quest to become a mom that I'd lost sight of how otherwise rich and multidimensional my life was. By vocalizing what I was thankful for, I reminded myself of the many other identities that I found great meaning in.

The next morning, I felt compelled to try to make something good out of the pain we were all feeling. I asked Haylee if she'd be comfortable with my sharing our experience on *A Slight Change of Plans*.

I wanted to convey my sincere appreciation for her. And I wanted to tell our collective story in the hope that it might help others who were in the throes of grief. Haylee was very supportive of the idea and said that she would find it healing. I asked my producer if he could interview me, ideally the following morning, before I had time to start stitching together a clean narrative. I wanted to give my listeners the gift so many of my guests had given me: unfiltered and unvarnished reflections.

In the days leading up to the release of the episode, I was nervous. I'd never shared something so personal with my listeners before. But after the episode came out, heartfelt messages began pouring in from around the world—from places like Greece, Mozambique, New Zealand, India, and Sweden. I was taken by how many of us, everywhere, have common stories—of feeling helpless, of questioning our decisions, of being swallowed up by grief, of struggling with our self-worth, of railing against life's cruelty.

Listeners opened up to me about their own, sometimes harrowing, experiences of loss. I heard from Jules, whose young and vibrant husband had died unexpectedly at the beginning of the pandemic, leaving her an unemployed single mom to three little boys. I heard from Erik, whose coworker had just lost her mom and her beloved dog; he'd told her to listen to this episode and was grateful that he could point her to something that might help her. And then there was Laura, whose twenty-one-year-old son had died of an accidental overdose. I was profoundly affected by stories like these.

I was moved, too, by the notes I received that were filled with love, empathy, and encouragement for Haylee, Jimmy, and me. I had set out to make meaning from my experience, to offer up my story in case it could help others. I didn't anticipate how much I would receive in return. I'd never before imagined what it would feel like to be hugged by the world all at once.

.

What happens after a change derails your dream? You might feel despair as the plans you'd so carefully laid out crumble in front of you. Perhaps you feel directionless, desperate to reclaim the sense of meaning you had when your life was oriented around the dream. You might experience frustration at how little control you had over how things turned out, envying those who got to their destination on the exact path they'd sketched out. Maybe you're left feeling like you simply didn't try hard enough. Or maybe you just feel depleted and filled with resentment. What was all that hustling, time, and emotional work for?

It occurred to Jimmy and me after the second miscarriage that the topic of kids had been the dominant focus of our relationship for six years now, seeping its way into even our most lighthearted conversations and imbuing our lives with a kind of heaviness. We'd been fully consumed by each step: working through my anxieties, researching adoption and surrogacy, enduring two egg retrievals, the ups and downs of the two pregnancies, and the heartbreak of losing Haylee as our surrogate. It had been a lot, and Jimmy insisted that we hit pause on our efforts to try to become parents so that we could recover some balance.

At first, I found the prospect of a break uncomfortable—my instinct was to keep charging forward. But the many interviews I'd conducted had taught me that change can reveal unexpected things to us, and unless we are intentional about reflecting on what they might be, they can go unnoticed. It was worth taking a moment to step back and process things for a bit.

In the time since, Jimmy and I have had many conversations about parenthood. Our embryos remain frozen at our clinic, and doctors have expressed optimism that things would likely work out if we partnered with another surrogate. We've also continued to learn from our friends who've gone through the adoption process. But the space we've given ourselves has also opened us up to conversations about *not* becoming parents. It's okay, we've realized, for us to revisit what we want for ourselves, even those things we were once certain about.

The first time Jimmy floated the idea of a child-free life, as we were sitting on the couch after work one evening, I was pleasantly surprised by my reaction. In contemplating the possibility, I no longer felt like my identity was under threat or that my life would be sapped of all its color and meaning. I still felt intact. I can't quite figure out when this shift happened. My best guess is that it was a gradual one, shaped in part by the many conversations I've had with people going through change.

As I move forward with this new perspective, I'm reflecting on how the people in this book have given me ways to think differently about the road ahead. Olivia, who found a way to reenvision her identity after being locked in, taught me about the benefits of creating a self-identity that is more resilient in the face of change. What exactly am I seeking from parenthood, and is it possible to find some of those same things elsewhere? Can I engage in the same mental exercise I used after losing the violin, but this time in the context of motherhood?

Inspired by Dwayne, who found a more expansive future for himself as a poet, I now feel empowered to author a new set of possible selves that don't include starting a family. As I do this, I see that, like Nora's early views on widowhood, so much of my thinking on this topic has been shaped by society's prejudices and the stigma attached to child-free women in particular. Similar to Ingrid, I've realized that some of the views I formed in childhood are worth revisiting.

I'm also channeling the internal evolution of Florence, who, in relinquishing her need for closure after the end of her marriage, taught me that there is some wonder in not knowing all the answers—in freely allowing parts of life to just unfold. I've discovered in writing this book how strong my desire for control and certainty is: I want to know not just how things will unfold but precisely how I will *feel* about those things. But decades of research show that we humans are notoriously bad *affective forecasters*: we simply don't make accurate predictions about how we will feel about specific events in the future. This is due to many cognitive biases, but among them is that we forget that we, too, will change over time, a phenomenon that the psychologist Dan Gilbert and his colleagues call the *end of history illusion*. And so, when I find myself creating overly detailed plans for my future, I try to remember that *I* will be a different person then, shaped by the many changes I happen to go through along the way.

In the meantime, I'm continuing to feed my love of human connection with the conversations I have with my friends and coworkers, and through my podcast guests and listeners. I'm also soaking up the affection and immeasurable happiness my six nieces and nephews give me—their snuggles, precocious observations about the world, and hilarious antics. A few moments come to mind: my nephew Eddie, age five at the time, proclaimed himself a "heartbreaker," and my niece Devi, then six, asserted that she wasn't whining but just "asking a question in a weird voice." At a recent family reunion, Jimmy and I were seated at the kids' table with my four oldest nieces and nephews—Stella, Vesper, Matteo, and Rohan—who ranged in age from six to eleven. Within minutes, we were sharing our biggest fears, our best days, and our most embarrassing moments. Whenever one of the kids' parents came within earshot, a hush would descend upon the table, all of us smiling knowingly at one another. After the meal, one of my brothers came over and jokingly interrogated Jimmy and me. "Tell me everything!" he exclaimed. Our lips were sealed.

I was going to be a violinist, and then I was going to be a mother. And now I find myself conceiving of a future in which I am neither. Unexpectedly, I'm more hopeful than I've ever been. I am slowly learning to hold my identity more loosely, with an open hand rather than a closed fist. Among the most valuable lessons I've learned from the people I've spoken with over the years is to stay curious when life makes other plans. Change can transform us in unexpected ways. We simply don't know how until we get there.

Appendix

Getting to the Other Side of Change:
Your Change Survival Kit

During the tough transitions in my life, I've wished that I had a companion of sorts—a guide to help me navigate my challenging emotions and start thinking and feeling differently. For those of you who, like me, appreciate having concrete strategies at your disposal that are backed by rigorous science, I've distilled some key concepts from each chapter below. Think of these not as rigid instructions but as a diverse set of instruments in your Change Survival Kit. How useful you find any given strategy may depend on the specific circumstances you're confronting. But my hope is that, no matter what you're going through, some combination of tools will help you see your situation from new perspectives and inspire you to reimagine who you can become. At the very least, I hope that this kit gives you the confidence that there *are* in fact more promising futures available to you, even if it takes you some time to discover what they might be.

Chapter 1: Revisiting our self-identity

WHAT THE SCIENCE SAYS

- When a big change happens in our lives, denial is a common reaction. It is a psychological immune response that can protect us from negative emotions like grief, guilt, fear, and helplessness. Denial can express itself in various ways: we might minimize the seriousness of a situation, project an overly optimistic view of the future, or engage in avoidance. Although denial can buffer us in the short term, it has downsides in the longer term.

- There are many causes of denial, including a threat to our self-identity, concerns that we, or our loved ones, lack the skills or resources to handle our new situation, a fear of social judgment, or shame over the decisions that we've made.

WHAT YOU CAN DO

- If you suspect that your denial is rooted in a threat to your self-identity, it can be helpful to ask if your identity is overly anchored to unstable sources over which you have little control. If so, can you tether your identity to more durable sources? For instance, is it possible to define yourself in terms of *why* you do something instead of just *what* you do?

- You can also engage in a **self-affirmation exercise** in which you actively shift your mental spotlight toward other aspects of your identity that you value, which are not threatened by the change you are going through. Self-affirmation can make you less susceptible to denial because it reminds you that your identity does not hinge entirely on what's been affected or taken away by the change. In doing so, it reduces the perceived intensity of the threat, enabling you to more openly embrace your reality.

Chapter 2: Revisiting what is possible in our future

WHAT THE SCIENCE SAYS

- When a big change happens in our lives, our set of **possible selves**—our ideas of who we can become—can shift dramatically. **Hoped-for selves** reflect our aspirations, **feared selves** embody our worries, and **expected selves** represent our predictions about what we think is most likely, good or bad.

WHAT YOU CAN DO

- In the face of unexpected constraints, one way to conjure up new, more positive possible selves is to tap into **moral elevation**. Moral elevation is the warm feeling you experience when you witness another person's moral beauty; it challenges your understanding of the world and cracks open your imagination about what is possible. You can invite moral elevation into your life by seeking out people's stories or by reflecting on remarkable acts of moral beauty you've encountered in the past.

- Another method for identifying new possible selves is to think about how the skills and knowledge you've cultivated may be relevant in different domains. Ask yourself: Who else can this person be?

- Once you've identified possible selves you'd like to bring into being, techniques informed by behavior-change research can help you actually realize those selves. For example, you can break big goals into smaller goals, thus avoiding the **middle problem**; take advantage of the **fresh start effect** by initiating goal pursuit at a time that naturally feels like a new beginning; and **temptation bundle** by pairing the behavior that you're finding challenging with a more immediately rewarding behavior. (You must deny yourself access to the rewarding behavior in any other context, so that it is exclusively paired with the challenging behavior.)

- You can also take advantage of the **peak-end rule**, which describes how, when we reflect back on an experience, we give greater weight to its emotional peak and its end. The upshot of this insight is that you can strategically shape your hedonic memory of an experience. For example, you might end a work session on a high note so that you're more likely to think back on it favorably and to return to your goal later on.

- Try to find or forge a community with people who believe in your new identity. Their shared vision can lift you when you're unsure of yourself, and reinforce your identity when you do succeed.

Chapter 3: Revisiting our mental patterns

WHAT THE SCIENCE SAYS

- When a big change occurs, our negative thoughts can take on a life of their own, nestling into our psyches and stoking our biggest fears. When we **ruminate**, we keep going over and over the same negative thoughts, and we get stuck in a loop. Our brains trick us into believing we're making progress on our problem when we're often just making things worse.

WHAT YOU CAN DO

- One of the best ways to break free from rumination is to actively zoom out—to engage in what is known as **psychological distancing.**

- There are many evidence-based ways to zoom out. **Cognitive reappraisal** involves reinterpreting your situation to alter its emotional impact. **Mental time travel** involves imagining the past or the future to see your problem from a different perspective. The experience of **awe** leads you to challenge your assumptions and to look beyond your individual wants, needs, and anxieties. **Affect labeling** is when you give your negative emotions a specific label—like "anger" or "sadness"—helping you mentally shift away from *being* the emotion to simply *having* the emotion. **Visual self-distancing** and **distanced self-talk** both involve gaining greater objectivity by taking a third-person point of view of your problem. **Distraction** can also be an effective tool; contrary to popular belief, it can be a healthy way to deal with the aftermath of a negative change.

- Loneliness and rumination often mutually reinforce each other, creating a vicious cycle. Being in community with others and seeing yourself reflected in their experiences can help you escape the cycle of rumination and open you up to valuable lessons those same people might teach you.

- Since discomfort with uncertainty and ambiguity can give rise to mental spirals, the more you can strive to exist comfortably in life's gray spaces and to lessen your need for **cognitive closure,** the less likely it is that rumination will take hold.

Chapter 4: Revisiting how we relate to others

WHAT THE SCIENCE SAYS

- A big change has the power to alter our relationships—distorting, straining, and sometimes breaking existing bonds. One way of understanding these dynamics is through a framework called **attachment theory**. There are three primary attachment styles: **secure, anxious**, and **avoidant**.

- Attachment styles are far more malleable than researchers once thought. They are not set in stone based on our early experiences; new life experiences can continually reshape them.

WHAT YOU CAN DO

- You can take deliberate steps to move toward a more secure orientation. Just as negative past experiences may have pushed you toward insecure attachments, new and positive experiences—with people who are reliable, and who make you feel comfortable and safe—can help you develop more secure attachments.

- You can also plumb your past and identify times when the people in your life showed up for you, cared for you, or protected you. In one study conducted over a four-month period, people who reflected each week on prior secure interactions saw a decrease in their levels of insecure attachment.

Chapter 5: Revisiting the beliefs we grew up with

WHAT THE SCIENCE SAYS

- Change can be an opportunity to reexamine our long-held beliefs, like those about our families. We might discover in the process that some of the beliefs we once thought of as sacred are actually worthy of revision.

WHAT YOU CAN DO

- Reexamining your beliefs involves cultivating **metacognitive awareness**, which is when you think *about* your thinking. Consider analyzing your ideas through the lens of a scientist: stay curious, question your assumptions, and treat your beliefs as hypotheses that should be tested. Ask yourself: How did I get from point A to point B in my thinking? Based on what existing beliefs did I form this new one? Would this belief hold up against the scrutiny of the people I trust? In theory, what evidence would persuade me to change my mind?

- Another way to unlock mental flexibility is to imagine that you were born during a different time, or into a different culture or family. Would you still have the same beliefs that you have now? What if you had been in a different emotional state when you first heard the information, or if the information had been delivered by a different messenger?

Chapter 6: Revisiting our beliefs about fairness

WHAT THE SCIENCE SAYS

- When we're grappling with a difficult, unwanted change, we might interpret what has happened through the lens of **a belief in a just world**. It can be comforting to think that the world is fair—that those who do good will be rewarded and that those who do bad will be punished.

- Thinking we have a big influence over how things turn out—having a strong **internal locus of control**—is a natural corollary to a belief in a just world. Research shows a correlation between a strong internal locus of control and greater well-being. But when inexplicable bad things happen, a strong locus of internal control can lead to undue self-blame and shame.

WHAT YOU CAN DO

- Reconsider how your belief in a just world might be affecting your responses to events in your life. What would it look like if you loosened your grip on this line of thinking?

- When a bad thing happens that is out of your control, one way to reduce any feelings of shame is to cultivate more **self-compassion**. Self-compassion involves, among other things, understanding that the pain you're feeling is part of a shared human experience. If you can contextualize an awful event in your life as something that can happen to other people, too, you're more likely to **depersonalize** it and interpret it as something that's happened *to* you, as opposed to something that's happened *because of* you. Engaging in self-compassion writing exercises and reorienting your focus toward helping others are both effective methods for boosting self-compassion.

Chapter 7: Becoming someone new on the other side of change

WHAT THE SCIENCE SAYS

- It is common to crave certainty when it comes to our future. But research shows we are bad **affective forecasters**; we don't make good predictions about how we will feel about specific events that haven't happened yet. In part this is due to a bias known as the **end of history illusion**, which says that we greatly underestimate how much we'll change in the future, even though we fully acknowledge that we've changed considerably in the past.

- As such, when we imagine what it will be like to navigate an unexpected change and its aftermath, it's easy to assume that we'll be the same person from beginning to end. We falsely believe that who we are right now is the finished product. But when a change happens *to* us, it can also create profound change *within* us.

- This is an empowering realization. When we're feeling daunted at the outset of a change, there is comfort in knowing that the person who will undergo the full experience will be different from who we are in this very moment. We will be a new person on the other side of change—in ways we are capable of shaping.

WHAT YOU CAN DO

- Stay curious and hopeful. You may be able to endure a negative change far better than you think, because you're underestimating your own ability to evolve as a result of that change. The relevant question to ask yourself isn't "How will I navigate this change?" but rather "How will I—with potentially new capabilities, values, and perspectives— navigate this change?" By and large the people I've interviewed have felt gratitude for the person they've become on the other side of change.

- Continue to stay connected with other people and their stories. I was familiar with most of the concepts in this book before writing it, but I wasn't able to fully internalize their value until I witnessed how they transformed the lives of the people I interviewed.

Acknowledgments

I feel profound gratitude for the people who were willing to be interviewed for this project. In addition to their generous time commitment, they regularly went to uncomfortable places and faced hard truths with the hope of helping us all. It is one of the greatest honors of my life to have been given a front-row seat to their exceptional stories and minds. My deepest thanks to the people profiled in this book: Olivia Lewis, Dwayne Betts, Matt Gutman, Tara Sharp, Ingrid Rojas Contreras, and Maryann Gray. It was a privilege to spend the final months of Maryann's life in conversation with her. Thank you also to Nora McInerny, Christine Hà, Kylie Yorke, Florence Williams, Ramsey Khabbaz, Brad Snyder, Scott, and Christy Warren, for allowing me to share your beautiful stories and enrich every chapter in the process.

Thanks to Courtney Young, my editor, who believed in me and the potential of this book before I had any idea what it could look like. There were many reasons I wanted you to be my editor—including your brilliant, logical mind and your ability to effortlessly switch between offering big-picture ideas and sentence-level edits—

but, let's be honest, it was this line from your letter after the book pitch meeting that made it a no-brainer: "Everyone came away from our meeting with giant cartoon hearts where their eyes used to be." Thank you, also, for waiting until I submitted my first round of revisions before telling me that you had panicked upon reading the first draft of the manuscript. Additional thanks to the entire team at Riverhead: Ashley Garland, Glory Anne Plata, Jynne Dilling Martin, Nora Alice Demick, Michelle Waters, Corinne Leong, Geoff Kloske, Helen Yentus, Grace Han, Caitlin Noonan, Randee Marullo, Lavina Lee, Patricia Clark, and Maureen Clark.

To my exceptional book agents at Creative Artists Agency: Dave Larabell and Anthony Mattero. You are so fantastic at what you do, and you've made me feel supported throughout this process. You were equally supportive, though, when I was just a person passionate about all things change, who pledged she would never, ever write a book. ;) Thank you to Kate Childs-Jones for her advocacy of this book and for helping me spread the word far and wide. Peter Jacobs: you are the best speaking agent I can imagine, full of such life, joy, good humor, and passion. I don't think I've ever left a conversation with you without a smile on my face. To Carly Fromm: you're the reason I got to be on TV with Chris Hemsworth—need I say more? And to Anna Jinks, thank you for helping me navigate the world of podcasting. My deepest gratitude to my podcast family <3: Tyler Greene, Britt Cronin, Megan Lubin, Kate PM, and Erica Cheung, and those in the broader Pushkin family, including Malcolm Gladwell, Gretta Cohn, Sara Nics, Eric Sandler, Kyra Posey, Amy Hagedorn, Morgan Ratner, Jordyn McMillin, Owen Miller, and Brian Srebrenik. A big shout-out to Katie Walton and Sigal Spitzer Flamholz for all of their strategic support to help me reach more people who might benefit from my work.

To the one-of-a-kind development editors Kate Rodemann, Chaz Curet, and Gareth Cook: what an honor it was to be your writing tutee over the past several years, and to learn how to craft narratives, assemble chapters, and write something besides an academic paper. You made writing a book an utter joy, and I feel delighted that I was able to build a new skill—one that I've discovered I truly love!— during this stage of my life. You are three of my most cherished intellectual collaborators, and I hope we go on to team up on other projects in the future. I also hope that we'll stay lifelong friends. Eli Mennerick: thank you for all your critical support behind the scenes, especially in the final stages.

I want to share my gratitude for my incredible team of research assistants, including Kylie Yorke (who knew you'd pull double duty as a character, too?!), Rachel Calcott, Stacey Kalish, and the formidable Alexandra Wormley, whose sharp mind and attention to detail allowed me to sleep easy knowing that my scientific references had been triple-checked for accuracy. Thanks also to the incredible set of freelance copyeditors who helped tame my own perfectionism by adding theirs to the mix! Naaman Zhou, Lauren Garcia, and Doug Watson—you are heroes, and I'm looking forward to taking a break from seeing the word "reppy." And of course to my fact-checkers Ben Kalin at FactCheckPros and Ismail Ibrahim for their diligence in vetting the contents of this book many times over for accuracy.

A heartfelt thanks to the academic community for their willingness to take impromptu calls or otherwise share their wisdom: Katy Milkman, Adam Grant, Dan Pink, Brené Brown, Molly Millwood, Dolly Chugh, Ethan Kross, Dacher Keltner, Annie Duke, Dan McAdams, Michael Pollan, Bruce Hood, Ximena Arriaga, Paul Bloom, Angela Duckworth, Dave McRaney, Gideon Yaffe, Charles Duhigg, Kieran Setiya, and Jonathan Adler. Thanks also to Meghan O'Rourke and Rachel Aviv for sharing their book-writing experiences with me. I want to also extend my gratitude to Suleika Jaouad, for role-modeling what it means to write with bravery and humility.

Thanks to my lifelong mentors, especially Laurie Santos. You took a chance on a seventeen-year-old who desperately wanted to join your monkey lab. Who knew all these decades later we'd still get to work together? You're the best mentor anyone could ask for. To Sam McClure, for taking me on as a postdoc and, just as significant, telling me that maybe academia wasn't the best fit for me. Richard Thaler, Cass Sunstein, and Tom Kalil gave me the opportunity of a lifetime to work in the Obama White House. To my musical mentors: Won-Bin Yim and Itzhak Perlman. And to Marie Gulin-Merle, Lorraine Twohill, and Philipp Schindler, who have long supported my BE-team ambitions. Michael Lewis: you've always believed in me and my potential far more than I ever thought reasonable. Thank you for being my biggest cheerleader. You and Tabitha have been truly wonderful friends to Jimmy and me.

To my amazing community of friends, who poured so much time and energy into reading drafts of this book at various stages along the way: Beth Foster, Raza Halim, Ben Rothenberg, Pravin Fernando, Shayak Sarkar, Aggy Djamanakova, Beth Zambrano, Jake Miller,

Casey Gardiner, Logan Chadde, Karina Livingston, Eshan Motwani, Jiyoung Han, Lesley Makishima, Karen Alper, Will Tucker, Hyunsoo Chang, Nate Higgins, Will Godel, Lauren Higgins, Anna Vogt, Sanghee Min, Christine Cha, Jonathan Wills, Ashley Jackson, Cole Scanlon, Scott Menke, Jules (hugs to her three adorable sons, Josiah, Jax, and Jude), Vivek Viswanathan, James Somers, and Sharon Traiberman. Matt Fuller, during the pandemic, your commitment to writing screenplays really inspired me to work hard on launching my podcast and everything that has followed. None of this would've happened without that role-modeling and your constant encouragement of my dreams (not to mention our epic workouts! ☺).

And to my family: my parents, Shankar and Uma; Jimmy's parents, Weijia and Bin; my dearest uncle and aunt, Ramkiji and Jeyamani; and Umesh, Angela, AJ, Bekah, Meera, Chris, Stella, Matteo, Vesper, Rohan, Devi, Eddie, and Nala. I love you to the moon and back.

And, of course, a very special thanks to Jimmy Li, who made massive contributions to this project. To have a built-in collaborator in my partner is not something I take for granted. Our working sessions were always filled with so much laughter and good cheer, even on my toughest days. Thank you for always helping me get unstuck, no matter how busy you were. There is no one whose opinion and judgment I respect more or hold more precious than yours.

When we got engaged, I told my friend Beth, "Marriage is like having a sleepover with your best friend every day for the rest of your life." Do you know how excited my younger self would have been if she'd known that you'd be part of her future? Loving you and being loved by you is the greatest, most endless source of joy in my life.

Notes

Preface

xii   *illusion of control:* E. J. Langer, "The Illusion of Control," *Journal of Personality and Social Psychology* 32, no. 2 (1975): 311–28.

xii   **have a 100 percent chance:** Archy O. de Berker et al., "Computations of Uncertainty Mediate Acute Stress Responses in Humans," *Nature Communications* 7 (March 29, 2016): 10996.

xv   *end of history illusion:* Jordi Quoidbach et al., "The End of History Illusion," *Science* 339, no. 6115 (January 4, 2013).

1: Locked In

3   **boyfriend from high school, Shawn:** Shawn is a pseudonym.

5   **called locked-in syndrome:** "Locked-in Syndrome (LiS)," Cleveland Clinic, my.clevelandclinic.org/health/diseases/22462-locked-in-syndrome-lis.

5   **like crying or laughing:** Simona Sacco et al., "Management of Pathologic Laughter and Crying in Patients with Locked-In Syndrome: A Report of 4 Cases," *Archives of Physical Medicine and Rehabilitation* 89, no. 4 (April 2008): 775–78.

6   **Bauby suffered a brain-stem stroke:** Jean-Dominique Bauby, *The Diving Bell and the Butterfly* (Alfred A. Knopf, 1997), 3–4.

6   muscles controlling his left eyelid: Bauby, *Diving Bell*, 4.

6   completed his memoir this way: Elizabeth Day, "A Story Told in the Blink of an Eye," *The Guardian*, January 27, 2008.

6   such as hugging his son: Bauby, *Diving Bell*, 71.

6   body is the diving bell: Bauby, *Diving Bell*, 5.

6   fewer than one thousand: "Locked-in Syndrome," Genetic and Rare Disease Information Center, last updated February 2025, rarediseases. info.nih.gov/diseases/6919/locked-in-syndrome.

6   never regain significant motor control: Taras Halan et al., "Locked-In Syndrome: A Systematic Review of Long-Term Management and Prognosis," *Cureus* 13, no. 7 (July 29, 2021).

7   diagnosis, from pneumonia: Thessaly La Force, "The False Widow," *New Yorker*, December 7, 2008.

11   a woman named Kate Allatt: Kate Allatt, *Running Free: Breaking Out from Locked-In Syndrome* (Accent Press, 2011).

13   varying degrees of intensity: Hanoch Livneh, "Denial of Chronic Illness and Disability: Part I. Theoretical, Functional, and Dynamic Perspectives," *Rehabilitation Counseling Bulletin* 53, no. 1 (2009): 44–55.

14   "we are dealing with flux": Richard S. Lazarus, *Fifty Years of the Research and Theory of R. S. Lazarus: An Analysis of Historical and Perennial Issues* (Lawrence Erlbaum Associates, 1998), 236.

14   experiencing *second-order denial*: Avery Weisman, *On Dying and Denying: A Psychiatric Study of Terminality* (Behavioral Publications, 1972), 67.

14   psychological immune response: Daniel T. Gilbert et al., "Immune Neglect: A Source of Durability Bias in Affective Forecasting," *Journal of Personality and Social Psychology* 75, no. 3 (1998): 617–38.

15   accepting our new reality: David K. Sherman and Geoffrey L. Cohen, "The Psychology of Self-Defense: Self-Affirmation Theory," *Advances in Experimental Social Psychology* 38 (2006): 183–242.

15   "much as we can handle": Elisabeth Kübler-Ross and David Kessler, *On Grief & Grieving: Finding the Meaning of Grief Through the Five Stages of Loss* (Scribner, 2005), 10.

15   during their hospital stays: Jacob Levine et al., "The Role of Denial in

Recovery from Coronary Heart Disease," *Psychosomatic Medicine* 49, no. 2 (March–April 1987): 109–17.

16 requiring more rehospitalization: Levine et al., "Role of Denial."

27 an approach called *self-affirmation*: Sherman and Cohen, "The Psychology of Self-Defense,"183–242.

28 drink less alcohol: Peter Richard Harris and Lucy E. Napper, "Self-Affirmation and the Biased Processing of Threatening Health-Risk Information," *Personality and Social Psychology Bulletin* 31, no. 9 (September 2005): 1250–63.

2: Possible Selves

35 men in nearby cells: R. Dwayne Betts, *A Question of Freedom: A Memoir of Learning, Survival, and Coming of Age in Prison* (Avery, 2009), 14–15.

35 commission of a felony: Betts, *Question of Freedom*, 65; *Commonwealth of Virginia vs. Reginald Dwayne Betts, Jr.*, Criminal No. 91580, Circuit Courtroom 5F, Fairfax County Courthouse, May 16, 1997.

36 headed to a shopping mall: Dylan Walsh, "'The Years That We've Lost,'" *Yale Alumni Magazine*, November/December 2022.

36 the following afternoon, on December 8, 1996: Betts, *Question of Freedom*, 45–46.

36 thirteen years in prison: Betts, *Question of Freedom*, 10; Walsh, "'The Years That We've Lost.'"

36 his state number, 91580: *Commonwealth of Virginia vs. Reginald Dwayne Betts, Jr.*

38 studying engineering at Georgia Tech: Betts, *Question of Freedom*, 50.

39 fourteen—named Jamil: Jamil is a pseudonym.

39 Dwayne's mind drifted to everything: Betts, *Question of Freedom*, 10, 50.

42 selves come in a number of forms: Hazel Rose Markus and Paula Nurius, "Possible Selves," *American Psychologist* 41, no. 9 (September 1986): 954–69.

44 **"I did not want that"**: Nora McInerny, interview by Maya Shankar, "When Surviving Is Enough," *A Slight Change of Plans*, November 7, 2022.

44 **rain and insects**: Walsh, "'The Years That We've Lost.'"

44 **"looked like a man-sized dog kennel"**: Betts, *Question of Freedom*, 164.

45 **birds flapping their wings**: Lydialyle Gibson, "An Obligation to Dignity," *Harvard Magazine*, October 6, 2021.

45 **vibrant underground library**: "Redefining Redemption by Finding Poetry in Prison," *Life Stories*, Kunhardt Film Foundation, September 15, 2022.

45 **fill pillowcases with books**: Freedom Reads, *Strategic Plan 2024–2026* (2023), 5.

46 **"create a new poetry"**: Dudley Randall, ed., *The Black Poets: A New Anthology* (Bantam Books, 1971), xxv–xxvi. Note: In keeping with Randall's original publication, the word "Black" is not capitalized in his quotations from *The Black Poets*.

46 **titled "For Freckled-Faced Gerald"**: Etheridge Knight, "For Freckle-Faced Gerald," in Randall, *The Black Poets*, 205.

48 **copied by hand**: Walsh, "'The Years That We've Lost.'"

48 **"albatross around their necks"**: Betts, *Question of Freedom*, 165.

48 **term for what Dwayne experienced** Jonathan Haidt, "The Positive Emotion of Elevation," *Prevention & Treatment* 3, no. 1 (March 7, 2000): Article 3c.

49 **"mercy on your soul"**: Dan McCullough, "Lessons from S.C. and Providence," *Providence Journal*, July 9, 2015.

49 **kind of "identity laboratory"**: Paul Ricoeur, *Oneself as Another*, trans. Kathleen Blamey (University of Chicago Press, 1992), 115; Jan Alber, "Literature as an Identity Laboratory: Storyworld Possible Selves and Boundary Expansions," *REAL* 36, no. 1 (December 2020): 57–71.

50 **try on new personality traits**: Alber, "Literature as an Identity Laboratory," 57–71; María-Ángeles Martínez, "Storyworld Possible Selves and the Phenomenon of Narrative Immersion: Testing a New Theoretical Construct," *Narrative* 22, no. 1 (2014): 110–31.

50 **"our personal identity"**: Cristina Loi et al., "On How Fiction Impacts

the Self-Concept: Transformative Reading Experiences and Storyworld Possible Selves," *Scientific Study of Literature* 12, no. 1 (2023): 44–67.

50   *The Language Instinct*: Steven Pinker, *The Language Instinct: How the Mind Creates Language* (William Morrow, 1994).

51   **eight-year sentence at the Indiana State Prison:** "Etheridge Knight," Poetry Foundation, https://www.poetryfoundation.org/poets/etheridge -knight.

51   **rumors that these guards had beaten:** Betts, *Question of Freedom*, 175.

51   **create a book using thread:** "Redefining Redemption," *Life Stories.*

52   **more than a thousand poems:** "Redefining Redemption," *Life Stories.*

52   **"When I'd gotten my first book":** Betts, *Question of Freedom*, 217.

53   **publish Dwayne's poem "A Different Route":** Betts, *Question of Freedom*, 218–20.

54   **"throwing that sandwich away":** Christine Hà, interview by Maya Shankar, "A Blind Cook Becomes a Master Chef," *A Slight Change of Plans*, August 18, 2022.

55   **"nuanced cook in the kitchen":** Christine Hà, interview by Maya Shankar, "A Blind Cook Becomes a Master Chef."

56   **calls the *middle problem*:** Ayelet Fishbach, "Motivation Isn't About Being Strong, It's About Being Wise," *Chicago Booth Review*, August 13, 2024.

56   **known as the *fresh start effect*:** Hengchen Dai, Katherine L. Milkman, and Jason Riis, "The Fresh Start Effect: Temporal Landmarks Motivate Aspirational Behavior," *Management Science* 60, no. 10 (October 2014): 2563–82; John Beshears, Hengchen Dai, Katherine L. Milkman, and Shlomo Benartzi, "Using Fresh Starts to Nudge Increased Retirement Savings," *Organizational Behavior and Human Decision Processes* 167 (2021): 72–87.

56   **known as *temptation bundling*:** Katherine L. Milkman, Julia A. Minson, and Kevin G. M. Volpp, "Holding the Hunger Games Hostage at the Gym: An Evaluation of Temptation Bundling," *Management Science* 60, no. 2 (2014): 283–99.

57   *peak-end rule*: Daniel Kahneman et al., "When More Pain Is Preferred to Less: Adding a Better End," *Psychological Science* 4, no. 6 (1993): 401–5.

58   **justice and preventing delinquency:** "President Obama Announces

More Key Administration Posts," White House, Office of the Press Secretary, April 16, 2012.

59 **when he received the letter:** Walsh, "'The Years That We've Lost.'"

59 **something he carried in the world:** "Redefining Redemption," *Life Stories.*

59 **more than four hundred libraries:** Freedom Reads website, freedomreads .org, accessed March 24, 2025.

60 **beautiful inside of a prison:** Walsh, "'The Years That We've Lost.'"

60 **writes in the first person:** Kathy Leonard Czepiel, "Acknowledgements," *Daily Nutmeg*, August 4, 2020.

60 **"barely see my daughters":** Dwayne Reginald Betts, "House of Unending," *Poetry*, April 2019.

3: Mental Spirals

62 **wearing his "lucky" underwear:** Matt Gutman, *No Time to Panic: How I Curbed My Anxiety and Conquered a Lifetime of Panic* (Doubleday, 2023), 5–6.

62 **was in physical danger:** Gutman, *No Time to Panic*, 4–5.

63 **"is simply devastating":** A. J. Katz, "ABC Suspends Matt Gutman After He Incorrectly Reported That All 4 of Kobe Bryant's Daughters Were on Helicopter with Him During Tragic Crash," *Adweek*, January 29, 2020.

64 **felt a "shame hangover":** Gutman, *No Time to Panic*, 4, 49, 89.

65 **This is known as *rumination*:** Randy A. Sansone and Lori A. Sansone, "Rumination: Relationships with Physical Health," *Innovations in Clinical Psychology* 9, no. 2 (2012): 29–34.

65 **not actually making progress:** Susan Nolen-Hoeksema et al., "Rethinking Rumination," *Perspectives on Psychological Science* 3, no. 5 (2008): 400–24.

66 **called *psychological distancing*:** Ethan Kross and Ozlem Ayduk, "Self-Distancing: Theory, Research, and Current Directions," *Advances in Experimental Social Psychology* 55 (2017): 81–136.

66 rumination's hamster wheel: Ethan Kross, interview by Maya Shankar, "The Science of Our Inner Voice," *A Slight Change of Plans*, August 30, 2020.

67 able to survive for so long: Gutman, *No Time to Panic*, 81–82.

68 miss a single real one: Randolph M. Nesse, "The Smoke Detector Principle: Signal Detection and Optimal Defense Regulation," *Evolution, Medicine, and Public Health* 2019, no. 1 (2019): 1; Gutman, *No Time to Panic*, 82.

68 detect social threats as well: Mark R. Leary, "Emotional Responses to Interpersonal Rejection," *Dialogues in Clinical Neuroscience* 17, no. 4 (2015): 435–41.

69 an example of *cognitive reappraisal*: Alexander D. Stover et al., "A Meta-Analysis of Cognitive Reappraisal and Personal Resilience," *Clinical Psychology Review* 110 (June 2024): Article 102428.

69 first-line treatments: Cope Feurer et al., "Emotion Regulation and Repetitive Negative Thinking Before and After CBT and SSRI Treatment of Internalizing Psychopathologies," *Cognitive Therapy and Research* 45, no. 6 (2021): 1064–76.

69 guided psychedelic trips: Gutman, *No Time to Panic*, 10–11, 161–67.

72 "before us than we imagine": Yuval Noah Harari, *Sapiens: A Brief History of Humankind* (HarperCollins, 2015), 241.

72 *mental time travel*: Thomas Suddendorf and Michael C. Corballis, "The Evolution of Foresight: What Is Mental Time Travel, and Is It Unique to Humans?," *Behavioral and Brain Sciences* 30, no. 3 (2007): 299–313.

72 exchange with a difficult coworker: Ethan Kross et al., "Self-Reflection at Work: Why It Matters and How to Harness Its Potential and Avoid Its Pitfalls," *Annual Review of Organizational Psychology and Organizational Behavior* 10 (2023): 441–64.

75 Loneliness can set off or intensify rumination: Dominik Borawski, "Authenticity and Rumination Mediate the Relationship between Loneliness and Well-Being," *Current Psychology* 40 (2021): 4663–72.

76 unresolved questions and unmended hearts: Florence Williams, *Heartbreak: A Personal and Scientific Journey* (W. W. Norton & Company, 2022), 260–64.

76 present in the narratives of others: Williams, *Heartbreak*, 260–64.

77 call *cognitive closure*: Donna M. Webster and Arie W. Kruglanski, "Individual Differences in Need for Cognitive Closure," *Journal of Personality and Social Psychology* 67, no. 6 (1994): 1049–62.

79 "The siren in my ear": Ramsey Khabbaz, interview by Maya Shankar, "Getting My Silence Back," *A Slight Change of Plans*, July 29, 2021.

80 "'enjoy it while it lasts'": *Hannah and Her Sisters*, directed by Woody Allen (1986; Orion Pictures).

81 experience of *awe*: Dacher Keltner, *Awe: The New Science of Everyday Wonder and How It Can Transform Your Life* (New York: Penguin Press, 2023).

81 associated with self-focus decreases: Michiel van Elk et al., "The Neural Correlates of the Awe Experience: Reduced Default Mode Network Activity During Feelings of Awe," *Human Brain Mapping* 40, no. 12 (2019): 3561–74.

81 individual wants, needs, and anxieties: Paul K. Piff et al., "Awe, the Small Self, and Prosocial Behavior," *Journal of Personality and Social Psychology* 108, no. 6 (2015): 883–99.

82 rooms faced a brick wall: Roger S. Ulrich, "View Through a Window May Influence Recovery from Surgery," *Science* 224, no. 4647 (April 27, 1984): 420–21.

82 "And that was inexplicable to me": Khabbaz, interview by Maya Shankar, "Getting My Silence Back."

83 kit is *affect labeling*: Jared B. Torre and Matthew D. Lieberman, "Putting Feelings into Words: Affect Labeling as Implicit Emotion Regulation," *Emotion Review* 10, no. 2 (April 2018): 116–24.

83 "fly on the wall" perspective: Kross et al., "Self-Reflection at Work."

84 *distanced self-talk*: Kross et al., "Self-Reflection at Work."

84 generating constructive advice: Kristin D. Neff, "Self-Compassion: Theory, Method, Research, and Intervention," *Annual Review of Psychology* 74 (2023): 193–218.

84 in the second person: Kross et al., "Self-Reflection at Work."

84 with even greater force: David K. Sherman and Geoffrey L. Cohen, "The Psychology of Self-Defense: Self-Affirmation Theory," *Advances in*

Experimental Social Psychology 38 (2006): 183–242; George A. Bonanno and Nigel P. Field, "Examining the Delayed Grief Hypothesis Across 5 Years of Bereavement," *American Behavioral Scientist* 44, no. 5 (January 2001): 798–816; Ethan Kross, *Shift: Managing Your Emotions—So They Don't Manage You* (Crown, 2025), 80–84.

84   recent research on resilience: George A. Bonanno, "Resilience in the Face of Potential Trauma," *Current Directions in Psychological Science* 14, no. 3 (2005): 135–38; George A. Bonanno, *The End of Trauma: How the New Science of Resilience Is Changing How We Think About PTSD* (Basic Books, 2021).

85   psychologist Ethan Kross writes: Kross, *Shift*, 88.

85   "the largest of feelings": Michelle Obama, *The Light We Carry: Overcoming in Uncertain Times* (Crown, 2022), 23.

4: A Hole in the Heart

95   framework called **attachment theory**: Mary D. Salter Ainsworth and John Bowlby, "An Ethological Approach to Personality Development," *American Psychologist* 46, no. 4 (April 1991): 333–41.

95   family members, friends, or acquaintances: R. Chris Fraley and Glenn I. Roisman, "The Development of Adult Attachment Styles: Four Lessons," *Current Opinion in Psychology* 25 (2019): 26–30.

95   three primary attachment styles: Mary S. Ainsworth, "Infant–Mother Attachment," *American Psychologist* 34, no. 10 (1979): 932–37.

95   stressful situations can activate: Jeffry A. Simpson, William S. Rholes, and Julia S. Nelligan, "Support Seeking and Support Giving within Couples in an Anxiety-Provoking Situation: The Role of Attachment Styles," *Journal of Personality and Social Psychology* 62, no. 3 (1992): 434–46.

96   combination of innate and environmental factors: Call with Ximena Arriaga, October 21, 2024.

96   shift our attachment style: R. Chris Fraley, Omri Gillath, and Pascal R. Deboeck, "Do Life Events Lead to Enduring Changes in Adult Attach-

ment Styles? A Naturalistic Longitudinal Investigation," *Journal of Personality and Social Psychology* 120, no. 6 (June 2021): 1567–1606.

112 **continually reshape them:** Fraley and Roisman, "Development of Adult Attachment Styles."

112 **"every relationship thereafter":** Faith Hill, "Attachment Style Isn't Destiny," *The Atlantic*, February 11, 2023.

112 **adult attachment style:** Fraley and Roisman, "Development of Adult Attachment Styles."

112 **"interpretation of them":** Hill, "Attachment Style Isn't Destiny."

112 **decreases in their attachment anxiety:** Nathan W. Hudson and R. Chris Fraley, "Moving Toward Greater Security: The Effects of Repeatedly Priming Attachment Security and Anxiety," *Journal of Research in Personality* 74 (June 2018): 147–57.

5: The Blank Slate

115 **Resistance groups were planting bombs:** *War Without Quarter: Colombia and International Humanitarian Law* (Human Rights Watch, 1998).

117 **word-of-mouth business:** Ingrid Rojas Contreras, *The Man Who Could Move Clouds: A Memoir* (Doubleday, 2022), 1–5.

118 **"with an ability to see":** Rojas Contreras, *The Man Who Could Move Clouds*, 5.

119 **difference between fiction and nonfiction:** Rojas Contreras appearance at Books Are Magic, July 20, 2022.

120 **sound of her skull hitting:** Rojas Contreras, *The Man Who Could Move Clouds*, 49.

121 **throw away her messenger bag:** Rojas Contreras, *The Man Who Could Move Clouds*, 52.

122 **it was just the adrenaline:** Rojas Contreras, *The Man Who Could Move Clouds*, 55–56.

123 **she had developed retrograde amnesia:** Caroline M. Roberts et al., "Retrograde Autobiographical Memory from PTA Emergence to Six-Month

Follow-Up in Moderate to Severe Traumatic Brain Injury," *Journal of Neuropsychiatry and Clinical Neurosciences* 31, no. 2 (2019): 112–22.

123 **degree of memory loss:** Peter Bright et al., "Retrograde Amnesia in Patients with Hippocampal, Medial Temporal, Temporal Lobe, or Frontal Pathology," *Learning & Memory* 13, no. 5 (2006): 545–57.

127 **"the sting of it was gone":** Rojas Contreras, *The Man Who Could Move Clouds*, 9.

129 **our *narrative identity*:** Dan P. McAdams, "Narrative Identity," in *Handbook of Identity Theory and Research*, ed. Seth J. Schwartz, Koen Luyckx, and Vivian L. Vignoles (Springer, 2011), 99–115; call with Dan McAdams, December 12, 2022.

129 **"I have essentially failed at my job":** Brad Snyder, interview by Maya Shankar, "Surrender Is Not in My DNA," *A Slight Change of Plans*, July 8, 2024.

130 **"To her, I was a badass":** Brad Snyder and Tom Sileo, *Fire in My Eyes: An American Warrior's Journey from Being Blinded on the Battlefield to Gold Medal Victory* (Da Capo Press, 2016), 152.

130 **"can't even get up to go to the bathroom by myself":** Snyder, "Surrender Is Not in My DNA."

133 ***Fruit of the Drunken Tree*:** Ingrid Rojas Contreras, *Fruit of the Drunken Tree* (Doubleday, 2018).

133 **"finally returned, learned anew":** Rojas Contreras, *The Man Who Could Move Clouds*, 271.

133 **chosen as a finalist:** National Book Foundation, "*The Man Who Could Move Clouds: A Memoir*," https://www.nationalbook.org/books/the-man-who-could-move-clouds-a-memoir/; The Pulitzer Prizes, "Finalist: *The Man Who Could Move Clouds: A Memoir*, by Ingrid Rojas Contreras (Doubleday)," https://www.pulitzer.org/finalists/ingrid-rojas-contreras.

134 **"start growing instead":** Emily Nagoski, *Come as You Are* (Simon & Schuster, 2021); Abby (Lombardo) Birk, "What Is 'Family of Origin' Work in Therapy?," Riverbank Therapy, riverbanktherapy.com/blog/2022/7/29/what-is-family-of-origin-work-in-therapy.

135 **mindset of a scientist:** Adam Grant, *Think Again: The Power of Knowing What You Don't Know* (Viking, 2021); Arnaldo Camuffo, Alessandro

Cordova, and Alfonso Gambardella, "A Scientific Approach to Entrepreneurial Decision-Making: Evidence from a Randomized Control Trial," Centre for Economic Policy Research, November 2017.

135 **beliefs that you carry now:** Grant, *Think Again*, 256.

6: A City of Refuge

NOTE: Maryann Gray shared hundreds of pages of her unpublished writing with me. Many of the details in this chapter are sourced from that writing.

140 **for the thirty-mile drive:** Alice Gregory, "The Sorrow and the Shame of the Accidental Killer," *New Yorker*, September 11, 2017.

143 **"It was an accident, Mommy":** Maryann Gray, unpublished writing.

144 *Handbook to Higher Consciousness:* Ken Keyes Jr., *Handbook to Higher Consciousness* (Living Love Center, 1972).

146 **"time you felt happy":** Maryann Gray, unpublished writing.

146 *just-world hypothesis:* Melvin Lerner, *The Belief in a Just World: A Fundamental Delusion* (Springer, 1980).

146 **they believe in a just world:** Zick Rubin and Letitia Anne Peplau, "Who Believes in a Just World?," *Journal of Social Issues* 31, no. 3 (1975): 65–90.

148 *locus of control:* Julian B. Rotter, "Generalized Expectancies for Internal Versus External Control of Reinforcement," *Psychological Monographs: General and Applied* 80, no. 1 (1966): 1–28; Holly S. Ryon and Marci E. J. Gleason, "The Role of Locus of Control in Daily Life," *Personality and Social Psychology Bulletin* 40, no. 1 (2014): 121–31.

148 **and greater well-being:** Kristina M. DeNeve and Harris Cooper, "The Happy Personality: A Meta-Analysis of 137 Personality Traits and Subjective Well-Being," *Psychological Bulletin* 124, no. 2 (1998): 197–229.

149 **on a rational level, he agreed:** Scott, interview by Maya Shankar, "Life After Surviving Stage Four Cancer," *A Slight Change of Plans*, March 6, 2022.

149 **"Was my old self that great?":** Scott, "Life After Surviving Stage Four Cancer."

150 **could not grant herself:** Maryann Gray, "The Day I Accidentally Killed a Little Boy," BBC, January 8, 2018.

150 **more than sixty had been injured:** Richard Winton and Martha Groves, "Case Is Closed on Deadly Day at the Market," *Los Angeles Times*, May 22, 2008.

151 **furious screams of "Murderer!":** Joel Rubin, Daren Briscoe, and Mitchell Landsberg, "Car Plows Through Crowd in Santa Monica, Killing 9," *Los Angeles Times*, July 17, 2003; Gray, "The Day I Accidentally Killed a Little Boy."

151 **elderly shoppers, and young children:** "Market Crash Victims Came from All Walks of Life," *Morning Journal*, July 18, 2003.

151 **small details of his life:** Maryann Gray, unpublished writing.

151 **struck by the strange behavior:** Lerner, *The Belief in a Just World*.

152 **disparage the victim:** Melvin J. Lerner and Carolyn H. Simmons, "Observer's Reaction to the 'Innocent Victim': Compassion or Rejection?," *Journal of Personality and Social Psychology* 4, no. 2 (1966): 203–10.

152 **victims of rape:** Adrian Furnham, "Belief in a Just World: Research Progress over the Past Decade," *Personality and Individual Differences* 34, no. 5 (2003): 795–817.

152 **"underlying moral order":** Rubin and Peplau, "Who Believes in a Just World?"

153 **five dollars on the street:** Kristina R. Olson et al., "Children's Biased Evaluations of Lucky Versus Unlucky People and Their Social Groups," *Psychological Science* 17, no. 10 (2006): 845–46.

153 **keep that belief alive:** Lerner, *The Belief in a Just World*, 9–30.

153 **"We're rescuers—that's who we are":** Christy Warren, interview by Maya Shankar, "First Responder's Call for Help," *A Slight Change of Plans*, October 10, 2022.

154 **he hadn't been faultless:** Note: Three years after the crash at the farmers market, Weller was convicted of ten counts of vehicular manslaughter with gross negligence and, after being deemed too ill to spend the remainder of his days in prison, was given five years' probation; Cindy Chang, "Elderly Driver Who Killed 10 Is Sentenced to Probation," *New York Times*, November 21, 2006.

155 **Within an hour:** Gregory, "The Sorrow and the Shame of the Accidental Killer."

155 **herself for the backlash:** Maryann Gray, "Commentary: Car Accidents," NPR, July 18, 2003.

157 **"another person must run":** Maryann Gray, unpublished writing.

160 **more self-compassion:** Kristin D. Neff, "Self-Compassion: Theory, Method, Research, and Intervention," *Annual Review of Psychology* 74 (2023): 193–218.

161 **decrease in shame:** Edward A. Johnson and Karen A. O'Brien, "Self-Compassion Soothes the Savage Ego-Threat System: Effects on Negative Affect, Shame, Rumination, and Depressive Symptoms," *Journal of Social and Clinical Psychology* 43, no. 6 (2013): 939–63.

161 **we form irrational beliefs:** Diana-Mirela Căndea and Aurora Szentágotai-Tătar, "The Impact of Self-Compassion on Shame-Proneness in Social Anxiety," *Mindfulness* 9 (2018): 1816–24.

161 **underestimate the positive impact:** Amit Kumar and Nicholas Epley, "A Little Good Goes an Unexpectedly Long Way: Underestimating the Positive Impact of Kindness on Recipients," *Journal of Experimental Psychology: General* 152, no. 1 (2023): 236–52.

162 **"value to bring to the world":** Vivek Murthy, interview with Maya Shankar, "The Science of Loneliness," *A Slight Change of Plans*, November 14, 2022.

7: The Missing Piece

168 **months away from having her ninth child:** *The Oprah Winfrey Show.*

170 **author Sheila Heti writes:** Sheila Heti, *Motherhood* (Henry Holt and Company, 2018), 95–96.

173 **makes reference to Room 101:** Salman Rushdie, *Knife* (Random House, 2024), 101–2.

173 **funniest people I know:** You don't have to take my word for it—a joke he

made in one of his physics lectures went viral and garnered tens of millions of views. ☺

174   **All suffering, however awful:** Maya Shankar, "The Joy of Being an Unwilling Traveler Through Life," *Meditative Story*, July 14, 2022.

189   **notoriously bad** *affective forecasters*: Timothy D. Wilson and Daniel T. Gilbert, "Affective Forecasting," *Advances in Experimental Social Psychology* 35 (2003): 345–411.

190   *end of history illusion*: Jordi Quoidbach et al., "The End of History Illusion," *Science* 339, no. 6115 (January 4, 2013): 96–98.

Index